Sherman Alexie

The Absolutely True Diary of a Part-Time Indian

Teacher's Manual

by
Ingrid Becker-Ross
and
Gunthild Porteous-Schwier

Contents

Teacher's Manual

Sherman Alexie · The Absolutely True Diary of a Part-Time Indian

Erarbeitet von
Ingrid Becker-Ross und Gunthild Porteous-Schwier
mit Dank an Radiana Ludwigs für wertvolle Anregungen aus ihrem Unterricht

Verlagsredaktion
Astrid Dany

Technische Umsetzung
Antje Kanniga

Umschlagfoto
© Shutterstock Images/nito

Herausgeber der Cornelsen Senior English Library
Prof. Dr. Albert-Reiner Glaap

www.cornelsen.de

1. Auflage, 2. Druck 2012

© 2010 Cornelsen Verlag, Berlin

Druck: Druckhaus Berlin-Mitte GmbH

ISBN 978-3-06-031264-1

 Inhalt gedruckt auf säurefreiem Papier aus nachhaltiger Forstwirtschaft.

Introduction

Reasons for Teaching the Novel

The Absolutely True Diary of a Part-Time Indian is one of those rare novels that can be enjoyed by young and old alike – and, as a novel for young adults, by both boys and girls. Although the story is told from an adolescent boy's point of view and deals with the importance of doing well on the sports team, female readers are bound to be intrigued by the protagonist's highly developed capacity for reflection and emotions, especially concerning friendship and loyalty. Besides, the character of Penelope, who certainly includes features for female readers to identify with, is given a considerable amount of attention in the story.

The novel is not too long even for fairly inexperienced readers, and the fact that many of the pages are made up of cartoons further illustrating the story will give these readers a welcome break. Other unusual formats, such as different types of lists, also break up the potential tedium of reading unrelieved prose. Of the 30 chapters in total, several consist of only a page or two, while others give accounts of exciting incidents in breathless detail over many pages.

There are other reasons why this novel lends itself so well to the successful teaching of extensive reading techniques, and in particular how to deal with unfamiliar vocabulary: The narrator's voice is that of a youngster speaking to other youngsters, i. e. informal and full of slang that is mainly self-explanatory within the context. Young readers will probably enjoy the wealth of slang here (especially the swear words), and soon realize when they do not need to fully understand a particular word in order to understand the message. The same goes for some of the specific basketball terms or the allusions to Native American culture. However, all these are annotated on first being mentioned so that students may deal with them more thoroughly if they wish.

One especially valuable aspect for the teaching of *The Absolutely True Diary of a Part-Time Indian* is the philosophical attitude toward life shown by the narrator and many of the people he quotes or refers to: There is obvious talk (and demonstration) of racism, alcoholism, poverty, violence and similar issues throughout the novel, giving students many opportunities to discuss the background of these issues and make up their own minds about some of the related incidents. The reflections of the protagonist-narrator prevent any black-and-white (or red-and-white!) clichéd view and can in fact help to promote an attitude of tolerance and respect toward others.

Perhaps the best feature of the novel for teaching is its humour, which will appeal to young adult readers because it prevents the plot from becoming moralizing and pretentious.

The fact that the novel is semi-autobiographical lends it credibility. This does not only apply to the protagonist's philosophical reflections on life, but also to the presentation of modern-day Native American culture. Students learn first-hand about contemporary life on a reservation, which for some may still be the stuff for adventure and folklore, and are given the chance to broaden their minds concerning life in relatively little-known areas of the United States.

Last but not least, it is a well-told story full of tension. First, some background facts about life on the "rez" are given which are important to appreciate much of the later plot. Then, the conflict of the "Part-Time Indian" is gradually unfolded and, through several critical events, brought to a satisfactory ending that still leaves scope for speculations on future developments.

General Remarks on the Suggested Teaching Approach

Students are bound to have some extensive reading experience in English by the time they have reached year 10, so they can be expected to apply their reading strategies to increasingly lengthy chunks of text as they progress through *The Absolutely True Diary of a Part-Time Indian*.

We suggest dealing with the first three chapters in class, largely under teacher guidance. However, while the discussion of these introductory chapters is still going on, students should start with the following sections, including the summaries (see our suggested reading chunks on p. 5). **Note:** During the reading stage, students will probably not be able to deal with additional written or creative homework, since they are expected to concentrate on reading and filling in the appropriate slots of their reading journals (see p. 5).

We suggest that they do a selection of the tasks on the worksheets in pair or group work during class time. Of course, with some of the tasks, classroom discussions may be called for.

When planning the time schedule, different types of readers should be taken into consideration. Students should be made aware of the pros and cons of slow vs. fast reading, as well as of the necessity of saving reference information during the lessons for later use.

The units suggested in this TM have been subdivided in order to help less experienced or less confident readers divide their reading into shorter stints. They have nevertheless been devised with an increasingly independent reader in mind. This means that students should be given all the copymasters of a unit at once and be encouraged to determine topics themselves. They can choose aspects of each unit and work individually or in smaller groups at their own pace, later sharing their work with their classmates.

Within the units, we have made suggestions for research topics and presentations. As a rule, it will not be possible to deal with all of these; rather, they constitute an opportunity for considered choices, as within the time frame available (about 6 weeks) teachers and students will have to agree on a limited selection of sub-topics.

The time available for dealing with the tasks on the novel may vary considerably, not least because student groups can be more or less experienced. Therefore, some of the tasks have been marked "Extra" to challenge the more experienced students, who need less time for the actual reading process.

Synopsis

Arnold Spirit, called "Junior" by his family and friends at home, lives in Wellpinit on the Spokane Indian Reservation as his family has always done. Born with brain damage, he unexpectedly survives an operation and several further physical handicaps, but he is always taunted and even beaten up for being a "retard".

Nonetheless, at the beginning of high school one of his teachers acknowledges that he is actually too smart for the reservation school and encourages him to leave. Arnold plucks up his courage and transfers to Reardan High School, which is just beyond the reservation border.

The novel is basically about his freshman year at Reardan, which is made even more difficult by the fact that he continues to live on the reservation, where he is now considered a traitor by most of the tribe, and especially by his former best friend Rowdy.

It takes Arnold a while to overcome the racism at Reardan, but gradually he makes friends, even "semi-dating" Penelope, the most popular girl in his class. Much of his success is due to his skill as a shooter in basketball

and the fact that the coach relies on him to improve the team. This, however, eventually leads to a personal confrontation with Rowdy as the best player of the Wellpinit team. After leading the Reardan team to victory against Wellpinit, Arnold suddenly feels ashamed for being on the winning side instead of with the "born losers".

During his freshman year, Arnold's beloved grandmother, his father's best friend Eugene, and worst of all, his sister Mary, who had left the reservation to marry a member of a different tribe and find a better life for herself, all die in alcohol-related accidents. This makes Arnold worry that he has put a curse on his family and tribe by leaving them and daring to dream bigger dreams.

It is through reading and reflection that he gradually accepts the fact that people have a right to pursue their own happiness, because their identity does not depend on only one group. His happiness is complete when he finds out that Rowdy is finally ready to accept that some Indians, like Arnold, have retained the nomadic streak they all used to have, and that they can still be considered friends.

Reading Journal

Early on in the reading process, students should be made aware of the need to save information and write down any questions they have while reading for later reference.

We suggest that each student individually fills in a kind of content table as a memory aid while progressing through the novel. They should be encouraged to make notes as opposed to attempting coherent chapter summaries. The content table can be done chapter by chapter (see model on pp. 8 ff.) or by using the subdivisions for each unit as suggested here (two or three chapters per subunit).

We also suggest that every student's reading journal should include unit summaries. However, this task can be shared in such a way that each student is ultimately responsible for only two such summaries. By writing the summary, the writer becomes an "expert" for the unit in question. The other summaries will be contributed by classmates. (The students sharing their summaries must put their names on them so that it is immediately obvious who is responsible for the work in the reading journal.)

A reading journal should also include answers to the chosen tasks suggested in the units. Some might need to be continued over more than one unit (e. g. character profiles), while others are short statements directly connected to only one chapter or unit (e. g. comments on character behaviour, explanation of a title, quote or cartoon), or they might aim at language practice (e. g. if-clauses about a particular event).

Some of the tasks involve preparing a presentation in class. This preparatory work should also be included in the reading journal.

Suggested Reading Chunks (Units And Subunits)

Unit 1 (p. 5 – p. 26): Getting to Know the Narrator
Ch. 1: The Narrator Himself
Ch. 2: The Parents
Ch. 3: His Best Friend Rowdy

Unit 2 (p. 27 – p. 52): Wellpinit School
Ch. 4/5: Mr. P And the Geometry Book
Ch. 6/7: Leaving Wellpinit High School

Unit 3 (p. 53 – p. 90): An Outsider in Reardan
Ch. 8–10: Coping
Ch. 11/12: Settling In

Unit 4 (p. 91 – p. 122): Gradual Acceptance in Reardan
Ch. 13/14: Family And Friends on the Rez
Ch. 15/16: Penelope
Ch. 17/18: Friends

Unit 5 (p. 123 – p. 163): Conflicting Loyalties
Ch. 19/20: Sister/Junior the Sportsman
Ch. 21–23: Red vs. White
Ch. 24: The Little Pieces of Joy

Unit 6 (p. 164 – p. 210): Coming to Terms
Ch. 25/26: The Match
Ch. 27: Mary's Death
Ch. 28–30: Remembering

Pre-reading Activities

The Cover – Looking at the Outside

Invite students to speculate (in small groups or with a partner) on the implications of the different elements of the title (what do they associate with "diary" and "part-time"; is the "absolutely true" phrase mere sensationalism or a promise of realism? Shouldn't diaries always be absolutely true? What might a "part-time Indian" be?)

Note:

– The blurb on the back cover might help to understand the "part-time Indian" of the title.
– The notes on the author (p. 212) can help to understand the meaning of "absolutely true".
– The title of the novel, "The Absolutely True Diary of a Part-Time Indian", could be taken literally as the author, Sherman Alexie, has drawn heavily on his own life for the character of Arnold Spirit, Jr. He too was born with hydrocephalus, and he too spent his childhood years in Wellpinit on the Spokane Reservation in the state of Washington, USA. And in his freshman year at the age of 14, Alexie also transferred from Wellpinit to Reardan High School. Against this autobiographical background, he manages to make us feel the "absolute truth" of the narrated experiences.

Ask students to brainstorm what they know about Native Americans and what they hope to find out in the novel, and to keep their notes in order to compare expectations and actual reading experience later.

Note:

– Either at the end of the discussion, or to trigger a critical approach, the following quote might prove helpful:

> "Indians call each other Indians. Native American is a guilty white liberal thing." (*Sherman Alexie*)

> (From: www.articlemyriad.com/biography_sherman_
> alexie.htm)

Ask students to describe what they see in the cover illustration, and to compare this with what they have brainstormed.

Speculating on the Basis of Quotes ➤ Copymaster 1

If students are already familiar with title and cover because they were involved in the selection process or have already been given basic information about the novel, the pre-reading activity on Copymaster 1 might prove a suitable alternative. It allows students to speculate on quotes deliberately taken out of context, thus initiating the discussion about certain aspects of the novel. This approach also demands that they look out for the context of these quotes as they read.

Possible answers:

1. Individual answers
2. Individual answers. The "pair" part can be done either with random partners, or, if the situation in the classroom allows, with partners having chosen the same (or mainly the same) quotes.
3. Individual answers. The "share" activity can result in a class poster similar to the one suggested above.

Looking at the Inside – Leafing Through the Book

Invite students to leaf through the book and comment on what strikes them.

Note:

– different chapter lengths, illustrations, layout, typeface, strange titles; no table of contents or numbered chapters
– This is a good opportunity for students to revise their vocabulary for describing books (as opposed to talking about novels).

Ask them to number the chapters for easier reference and orientation when working out reading chunks and details of their reading journal.

Speculating on the Basis of Quotes

TASKS

1 Think: Choose two or three quotes that you would like to speculate on: What does the sentence mean? What kind of context can you imagine for it?

2 Pair: Explain your choice of quotes to each other and compare choices. Discuss: What attitude toward life do they suggest? What questions do they give rise to? Make notes.

3 Share (in class): Collect the information gathered from the quotes, and list what kind of story it makes you expect, and what questions you hope will be answered. Save your notes.

"I am a zero on the rez." (p. 19, l. 1)

"Who has the most hope?" (p. 46, l. 4)

"We were supposed to kill the Indian to save the child." (p. 36, ll. 31–32)

"He was the loser Indian father of a loser Indian son living in a world built for winners." (p. 54, ll. 1–2)

"It was like being Indian was my job, but it was only a part-time job. And it didn't pay well at all." (p. 109, ll. 4-5)

"If you let people into your life a little bit, they can be pretty damn amazing." (p. 119, ll. 21–22)

"You have to dream big to get big." (p. 126, l. 7)

"We Indians really should be better liars, considering how often we've been lied to." (p. 13, ll. 17–18)

"I mean, you have to love somebody that much to also hate them that much, too." (p. 174, ll. 18–19)

"You are a good kid. You deserve the world." (p. 42, l. 1)

Working With the Individual Chapters

Chapter-by-Chapter Content Table

Note: Narrated action that does not fit into the chronology of events has been marked *italic*.

Chapter (pp.)	Who?	When?	Where?	What?
1: The Black-Eye-of-the-Month Club (5–10)	Junior (Jr.)	first 14 years of his life	on the rez	brain damage at birth, too many teeth, lopsided glasses, gets beaten up and is called "retard" (p. 8, l. 13), draws cartoons
2: Why Chicken Means So Much to Me (11–17)	Jr., dog Oscar, Dad, Mom	last week	on the rez	Family too poor to afford a vet, father has to shoot his son's "best friend" (p. 12, l. 13), the dog Oscar, when he gets too sick. Junior devastated. (Chicken: KFC)
3: Revenge Is My Middle Name (18–26)	Rowdy, Jr.	shortly after	on the rez / at the powwow	Rowdy born "mad" (p. 20, l. 19), beats everybody up, but protects Jr. against attacks from others; cuts off the braids of three men who bullied Jr. at the powwow; they are inseparable.
4: Because Geometry Is Not a Country Somewhere Near France (27–33)	Jr., Mary, Mr. P	first day of high school	on the rez, at school	Jr. excited about high school and especially geometry, but is so frustrated when he sees that they are using the same books their parents used that he throws his and hits Mr. P on the nose. (His sister Mary lives in the basement, hiding from the world ever since she graduated from high school.)
5: Hope Against Hope (34–44)	Jr., parents, grandmother, Mr. P, (Mary)	shortly after	at Jr.'s house	Jr. is suspended from school after the incident, family ashamed of him, Mr. P comes to visit, tells Jr. to leave for a better school because he is too smart for this one, deserves more hope. Says Mary was even smarter than him, wanted to write romance novels, but is too ashamed so she hides in basement.
6: Go Means Go (45–47)	Jr., parents	directly after	at Jr.'s house	Jr.'s parents allow him to transfer to Reardan High School immediately, although R. is known as a racist town.
7: Rowdy Sings the Blues (48–52)	Jr., Rowdy	next day	rez school playground	Jr. tells Rowdy he's leaving, wants him to come as well, but R. is furious and turns from best friend to worst enemy.
8: How to Fight Monsters (53–63)	Jr. (=Arnold Spirit), Dad, school secretary, teacher, Penelope, some senior boys (Roger)	next morning, that week on the 7th day at lunchtime	Reardan High School	Jr. is the new boy, stared at and then ignored or called insulting names. He is the only Indian at the school, apart from the mascot, a statue of an Indian; is intrigued by Penelope, who ignores him after the first day; on the 7th day, a group of seniors tell him an insulting racist joke, and he hits Roger in the face. Roger does not fight back (i.e. does not act according to the "Rules of Fisticuffs", p. 59) and Jr. fears for his life.

Chapter (pp.)	Who?	When?	Where?	What?
9: Grandmother Gives Me Some Advice (64–69)	Jr., grandmother, Eugene, Roger, Penelope	that evening, next morning	Jr.'s home; way to school, at Reardan	Grandmother tells him the others will now respect him because he hit the "alpha male" (p. 66, l. 19). Eugene, though drunk, gives him a ride to school on his vintage motorbike; Roger shows respect; Penelope still ignores him.
10: Tears of a Clown (70–71)	*Jr., Rowdy*	*2 years earlier*	*on the rez*	*Jr. confesses to Rowdy that he has fallen in love; Rowdy refuses to take that seriously, but never tells anybody about it.*
11: Halloween (72–75)	Jr., Penelope, some Indian boys	Halloween ("today", later that night, the next morning)	Reardan, on the rez, back at school	Jr. and Penelope both dressed up as homeless bums; P. wants to raise money for real homeless people, agrees to let Jr. join her; Jr. gets beaten up, the attackers take away his money; P. feels sorry for him next day, but they don't become closer yet.
12: Slouching Toward Thanksgiving (76–90)	Jr., science teacher, Gordy, Mary	the next few weeks	Reardan, home	Jr. is lonely, isolated, knows about petrified wood, teacher doesn't believe him, but Gordy (class genius) corroborates his theory; the boys become friends of a sort (study together). Mary runs away, marries a Flathead Indian in Montana.
13: My Sister Sends Me an E-mail (91–92)	*Mary*	*Nov 16, 2006*	*Montana*	*Mary loves her new life, is happy.*
14: Thanksgiving (93–95)	Jr., family, Rowdy's dad, Rowdy	Thanksgiving	on the rez	Perfectly cooked turkey dinner; Jr. misses his friend Rowdy, draws him a cartoon and asks his father to give it to him; sees R. giving him the finger at the window: but he didn't tear up his cartoon.
15: Hunger Pains (96–105)	Jr., Penelope, P.'s father, the other kids	one school morning	at school	Jr. goes to the bathroom during class time, hears Penelope vomiting and they talk about bulimia; start semi-dating. P.'s father is racist and warns Jr. off; the others are intrigued. P. tells Jr. about her dreams.
16: Rowdy Gives Me Advice About Love (106–108)	Jr., Penelope, Rowdy, Gordy	"Yesterday"	Reardan, home	Jr. is in love with P., asks Rowdy for advice via e-mail: R. tells him he is a racist; Gordy tells him the same thing.
17: Dance, Dance, Dance (109–119)	Jr., Penelope, Roger, other kids	at the Winter Formal Dance	Reardan	Jr. and P. enjoy the evening, Jr. manages to hide the fact of his poverty at first, but later Roger guesses it, and helps him out without condescension. Penelope stays his friend.
18: Don't Trust Your Computer (120–122)	Jr., (Rowdy), Gordy	"Today"	at school, computer lab	Jr. mails a picture of his smiling face to Rowdy, who mails back one of his bare ass; Gordy sees it; they talk about weird people threatening the safety of the community.
19: My Sister Sends Me a Letter (123–124)	*Mary*	*unspecified*	*Montana*	*Wants to write a book about "How to run away from your house and find a home".*

Chapter (pp.)	Who?	When?	Where?	What?
20: Reindeer Games (125–137)	Jr., Dad, Coach, Roger the Giant, Rowdy and the tribal members	beginning of sports season, two weeks later	home, Reardan, on the rez	Dad encourages Jr. to "dream big" (p. 126, l. 7). Jr. makes the varsity team (holds his own against Roger during tryouts). The big match between Reardan and Wellpinit on the rez: Rowdy knocks Jr. unconscious, and Wellpinit wins. Coach visits Jr. in hospital and they share stories.
21: And a Partridge in a Pear Tree (138–139)	Jr., Dad	Christmas holidays	home	Jr. gets a five dollar bill from his dad, who spent Christmas drunk and away from home.
22: Red Versus White (140–145)	Jr., (Mary), grandmother, (parents, Gerald the drunk driver)	last week	on the rez	(General remarks on loving Indians and Whites, and postcards from Mary) Grandmother is run over and killed by a drunken driver. She was always tolerant and forgiving, she forgives the driver before she dies.
23: Wake (146–154)	Jr., about 2000 Indians, Billionaire Ted, Mom	3 days later	on the rez	During the funeral rituals, Ted makes a speech about a powwow dancing outfit that belonged to Grandmother Spirit and that he wants to give back to her family; Mom looks at it, and says it couldn't have belonged to her mother, because she never danced at powwows, and it wasn't Spokane at all. That makes all the Indians laugh (and cry at the same time).
24: Valentine Heart (155–163)	Jr., Eugene, teacher, Gordy, Penelope, class friends*	a few days after Valentine's Day, a few weeks after that	(rez) Reardan High School	Eugene is shot dead in a drunken fight. Jr. believes he has cursed his family and tribe for going to Reardan, and drops out for 15–20 days. When he goes back, his teacher mocks him, but his classmates stand by him by leaving her class. He makes lists of the things and people that give him joy in life.
25: In Like a Lion (164–180)	Jr., Coach, team members (esp. Rowdy), camera guys, spectators (esp. parents/ Dad looking serious)	later in the season, the night of the rematch with Wellpinit	Reardan gym	Jr. is expected to be good and wants to live up to expectations. He is to cover Rowdy during the whole rematch. Before the match, he annoys the TV team by not wanting to go public with his real feelings, but he manages to express himself. With superhuman effort, he beats Rowdy in the first 10 secs. of the game, Reardan wins by 40 points; in the end, Jr. is ashamed of having led the white team to victory against his own people.
26: Rowdy and I Have a Long and Serious Discussion About Basketball (181)	Jr., Rowdy	after the basketball season	---	Jr. apologizes, Rowdy threatens revenge; Jr. is happy because R. actually answered.

*Editorial note: incl. Roger, although he's definitely not a freshman like Arnold and Penelope (p. 114, ll. 1 f.)

Chapter (pp.)	Who?	When?	Where?	What?
27: Because Russian Guys Are Not Always Geniuses (182–195)	Jr., school staff, Dad, extended family, Rowdy	"today, around 9 a.m." (p. 183, l. 11), deep winter	Reardan, the rez, Reardan again	Jr. rejects Tolstoy's statement that all families' unhappiness is different. Indians' unhappiness always stems from alcohol: his sister Mary burned to death in a trailer when she was drunk. After the funeral, Rowdy, weeping, accuses him of having killed her by going away; back at Reardan, his friends show real sympathy and acceptance.
28: My Final Freshman Year Report Card (196)	---	(end of school year)	---	Parody of a report card (with mainly As, which might be true…)
29: Remembering (197–199)	Jr., parents	"today"	on the rez: the graveyard	Cleaning the graves, experiencing love and harmony within the family, missing Rowdy; coming to terms with who he is and where he belongs.
30: Talking About Turtles (200–210)	Jr., Rowdy	*summer, when the boys were 10; present summer vacation*	*on the rez: Turtle Lake, the pine tree* home	*Jr. remembers a hot day when they climbed the highest pine tree instead of swimming in Turtle Lake.* Rowdy comes home, they discuss R.'s coming to Reardan with him. R. explains that only Jr. has retained the nomadic Indian streak. They play one-on-one basketball without keeping the score.

Preliminary Note

The narrator and protagonist of the novel is a 14-year-old boy called "Junior" on the reservation, and "Arnold" at his new school in Reardan (cf. chapter 8). It might prove helpful to tell the class at least about the name "Junior" at some stage in Unit 1, although as readers we do not learn about it before the boy is asked his name on his first day at Reardan High School. However, using a name makes talking about the events easier. In this TM, the name "Junior" has primarily been used for situations on the reservation, and "Arnold" for situations in the white community of Reardan.

> **Hydrocephalus**
> The word comes from Greek "hydro" (water) and "cephalus" (head), and is sometimes referred to as "water on the brain". Affected infants usually develop a strikingly large head because the skull bones are pushed outwards (cf. German "Wasserkopf"). When hydrocephalus occurs in adulthood, the skull bones are no longer flexible, so too much pressure builds up in the brain, leading to convulsions and mental retardation. If children are treated properly, i.e. the fluid is transported from the central nervous system to the blood, they will not suffer from mental disabilities.

Unit 1: Getting to Know the Narrator

Summary

The first three chapters offer a kind of exposition to the plot. We learn that the narrator was born with hydrocephalus and a series of other physical handicaps, and that these inevitably lead to his getting beaten up all the time by not only his peers but also some older Indians. His family is very poor, so that they cannot afford a vet to cure the narrator's dog and have to shoot him instead. However, it becomes clear that this is done out of love, and the narrator feels this, although he is devastated. In contrast, his best friend, Rowdy, comes from an equally poor, but less loving family and suffers beatings from his alcoholic father. Rowdy is tough and protects his friend from bullies.

Chapter 1 (The Narrator Himself) ➤ Copymaster 2
Possible answers:
1. Individual answers
2. He exaggerates, uses strong metaphors ("water on the brain" p. 5, l. 1, "mucked up the works" l. 8, "drowning in grease" l. 10, "brain as a giant French fry" l. 12); he makes his handicap sound funny, although he admits that his relatives did not find it funny when he had to be operated (p. 6, ll. 3–6).
   The tone is humorous, but the actual message is serious. However, the narrator is quick to point out that it can't be all that bad because he is there to tell the story (p. 6, ll. 11/12).
3. Physical problems:
   - hydrocephalus (p. 5)
   - 42 teeth instead of 32 (p. 6, ll. 14/15)
   - one nearsighted and one farsighted eye, causing headaches (p. 7, ll. 3–6)
   - wearing glasses (p. 7, l. 9)
   - skinny, but with huge hands and feet (p. 7, ll. 11/12)
   - "enormous skull" from the hydrocephalus (p. 7, l. 15)
   - speech impediments: stutter and lisp (p. 8, l. 3)

4. (Extra) Individual answers
5. There is a club called "Book-of-the-Month-Club", sending members one particular book a month; Alexie here uses the title to stress that his narrator is in a club that gives him at least one black eye a month. (p. 8, ll. 24-27)
6. Drawing gives him more scope than words, which are limited, unpredictable and only understood by the speakers of the particular language used, while his cartoons can be universally understood (cf. p. 9). Besides, being able to draw makes him feel important (p. 10).
7. Individual answers
8. (Extra) In a world full of danger and risks, the cartoons are a means of escaping the dangers and avoiding the risks by communicating without words.

Chapter 2 (The Parents) ➤ Copymaster 3
Possible answers:
1. Oscar, the narrator's little dog, suddenly became very sick and was in obvious pain. He was having seizures, was vomiting and had diarrhoea, but the family had no money to take him to a vet. So the narrator's father shot him to put him out of his misery. (48 words)
   a) Individual answers
   b) The narrator stresses the emotional importance of the dog as his best friend. He gives details of what the dog is going through and the pain he feels. He shows his own sense of helplessness and fury at his father's solution; we feel the narrator's mental anguish at losing his best friend.
2. He lives in utter poverty, he is not able to save another creature from illness. He's emotional about the situation, but also understanding and he tries to be fair; he mentions his mother hugging him and showing her sadness (p. 13, l. 29), also his father's sadness (p. 14, l. 22). He loves his parents and understands why they are poor (because they are reservation Indians, p. 16, ll. 20 ff.).

Read pp. 5–6 (l. 13) and try to understand what you read with the help of the annotations.

TASKS   1   Tell each other what you have understood. Note down what further information you need to understand better what's physically wrong with the narrator.

2   In class, discuss how the narrator writes and talks about himself, and how you feel reading and talking about it.

> Language help to talk about your feelings:
> It's embarrassing – it makes me feel awkward – I was shocked / taken aback – it made me laugh although it's really bad/sad – I was impressed by the directness – it upset me to read about – I identified with the narrator when – I felt sad/happy for the narrator when – I particularly enjoyed reading/learning about – I sympathised with the character

Read on up to p. 8, l. 16.

3   Make a list of the physical problems mentioned.

4   **(Extra)** Compare your list with a partner and tell each other what you personally think about this boy and how you might react if you met someone like him.

Finish reading the chapter (p. 10).

5   Explain the title of the chapter.

6   Explain why the narrator draws cartoons (as well as writes) about himself.

7   Choose one of the two drawings and describe what you see and what effect it has on you.

8   **(Extra)** "I think the world is a series of broken dams and floods, and my cartoons are tiny little lifeboats" (p. 10, ll. 10 f.). Explain this metaphor.

Read all of chapter 2 in one go.

TASKS

1 With a partner, write a short summary of what happened to Oscar (40–60 words).
    a) Listen to a few summaries in class, and compare the effect of these with the way you felt when you read the episode as told by the narrator.
    b) Discuss how the author achieves this effect. Save your results in your reading journal.

2 Explain what this episode shows us about the living conditions of the narrator and his family, and about his relationship with his parents.

3 What does the narrator tell us about his parents and their dreams? With a partner, study the cartoon on page 15 as well as the text on page 14, line 31, up to the end of chapter 2.
   One of you sums up all you know about the mother, and the other all about the father. Write in your own words. Save your results in your reading journal.

4 **(Extra)** What do you know about your parents' dreams? Write a short text about their dreams and whether they have been able to realize them, and put it in your reading journal.

5 Look at the title of chapter 2, and explain what it means in connection with all you have already found out about this chapter.

6 The narrator says his favourite food is Kentucky Fried Chicken (p. 12). What is yours?
   Describe what you particularly like about it, and compare your description with the narrator's description of KFC.

3. Mother: Would have liked to go to college; an avid reader who remembers what she reads and can recite it from memory, including disparate information from the newspaper (p. 16, ll. 7–13).
   Father: wanted to become a musician; still sings when drunk, and sounds good; plays the guitar and a bit of piano, and keeps his old saxophone from high school clean and shiny (p. 16, ll. 14–19).
4. (Extra) Individual answers
5. The chapter deals with the topic of poverty, and with the fact that hunger is not the greatest problem when you are poor (as there will always be a bit of chicken), but rather that a poor family cannot afford the vet to save a suffering dog (p. 12, ll. 8 ff.).
6. The narrator's favourite food is KFC, and apparently that is something the family can afford from time to time. Especially when they have gone hungry all day, he says, "a good piece of chicken can make anybody believe in the existence of God" (p. 12, ll. 6 f.).

Chapter 3 (His Best Friend Rowdy) ➤ Copymaster 4
Possible answers:
1. Notes on Rowdy:
   - "the toughest kid on the rez" (p. 18, l. 7)
   - obviously physically fit ("long, lean and strong") (p. 18, ll. 7/8)
   - mentally tough and up to every trick ("heart as strong and mean as a snake" p. 18, l. 9)
   - has been acting violently and aggressively all his life, fighting everybody and everything (p. 20, ll. 20 ff.)
   - born on the same day as Jr. (p. 20, l. 17)
   - his name is a telling name (cf. OALD "rowdy": making a lot of noise or likely to cause trouble)
   - his father is an alcoholic who beats Rowdy and his mother (p. 19, l. 8)
   - spends a lot of time in Junior's house (p. 19, ll. 29/30)
   - almost like a brother because he wants to flee his own miserable living conditions at home (p. 19, l. 30)
2. Rowdy and Junior:
   - Rowdy always protects Junior (p. 20, l. 16)
   - R. is Jr.'s "best human friend" (p. 18, l. 10)
   - they are "inseparable" (p. 26, l. 32)
   - spend a lot of time together (p. 26, ll. 25/26)
   - know each other's dreams and fears (p. 26, ll. 15 ff.)
   - they care for each other, they trust each other and they enjoy each other's company despite their obvious differences and problems (different family background with regard to love and acceptance, but both have fathers with a drinking problem; R. is strong and physically tough, aggressive, J. is physically handicapped and vulnerable, behaves like a 'loser')

3. Possible quotes:
   - "I draw his dreams" (p. 26, l. 14);
   - "I think Rowdy might be the most important person in my life." (p. 26, l. 18)
   - "He is the only person who listens to me." (p. 22, l. 4)
4.

Junior	shared space	Rowdy
physically handicapped	best friends	physically strong
weak	live on the rez as Spokane Indians	aggressive
is loved by his parents	like comics	gets hurt by his father
draws comics	talk about their dreams	---

5. (cf. OALD "middle name": used to say that sb. has a lot of a particular quality) Rowdy's middle name in this sense is "Revenge": he revenges himself on anyone who hurts either him or his best friend.

End of Unit 1 ➤ Copymaster 5
Possible answers:
1. Indian terms:

Reservation ("rez")
Area of land allotted to different Native American tribes by white authorities in the 19th century. Today, over half of the Native Americans in the USA live outside reservations, mainly in large western cities. Reservations are partially self-governed. The Bureau of Indian Affairs (BIA), a Federal government agency, constitutes the link between the tribal governments and the US government. It is responsible for all "Indian affairs" except health, for which the Indian Health Service (IHS) was created as an agency within the US Department of Health and Human Services.

Powwow Celebration
A special Native American celebratory event. Native American, but also non-Native American people come together to have a good time dancing, singing and enjoying each other's company. Pow-wow celebrations can last between about 5-6 hours up to a whole week.

Spokane Indians
A Native American tribe in the north-eastern part of Washington State. The name literally means "children of the sun", or "Sun People".

2. hunger – poverty; family – friendship; physical handicaps – violence; revenge – alcohol
3. cf. summary on p. 12

TASKS 1 While reading chapter 3, make short notes on Rowdy, his family and their living conditions. Start a character profile of Rowdy and add to it whenever you come across new information.

2 On the basis of your notes, discuss the friendship between Rowdy and the narrator in groups of 3–5, concentrating on the question how the two deal with each other, their problems and differences.

3 In your group, agree on two quotes from the chapter that best illustrate the friendship, and explain your choice to the rest of the class.

4 Fill in the diagram below to show what common traits Rowdy's and Junior's friendship is based on.

5 Look up "middle name" in your dictionary and see if it can help you explain the title of the chapter (in your reading journal).

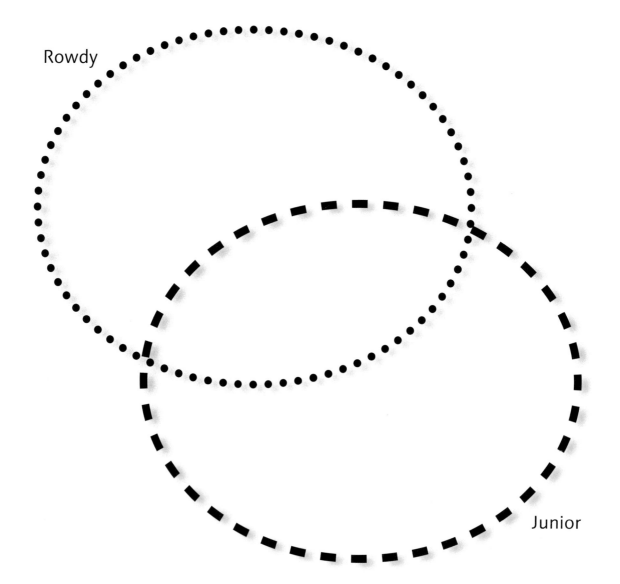

Rowdy

Junior

TASKS

1 As part of your reading journal, start a list of terms referring to Indian life (e. g. "rez"), to be continued while reading the rest of the novel. Make sure you can explain what each term means. You might want to find out more about some of the things mentioned using the Internet. Some sites have illustrations that you might want to save in your journal.

2 List the topics dealt with in the first three chapters and discuss how some of them relate to each other (e. g. hunger and poverty) in small groups.

3 Write the unit summary.

Unit 2 (pp. 27–52): Wellpinit School

Summary

On his first day of high school, which he has been looking forward to, Junior gets so frustrated when he realizes that they will be using the same books their parents used, that he throws his geometry book across the classroom, hitting his teacher on the nose. Consequently, Junior gets suspended but while he is off school, his teacher visits him at home and explains that if he wants a better life he will have to leave the reservation. As a result, Junior decides to transfer to the high school in Reardan outside the reservation. This, however, causes Rowdy to accuse him of being a traitor and turn his back on him in disgust.

Chapters 4/5 (Mr. P And the Geometry Book)
➤ **Copymaster 6**
Possible answers:

1. Individual answers
2. Suggestions for reading passages:
   - surprising/sad: p. 32, l. 10 – p. 33, l. 7 (the geometry book)
   - funny: p. 38, l. 20 – p. 39, l. 18 (on romance novels)
   - interesting/unexpected: p. 36, l. 27 – p. 37, l. 13 (Mr. P); p. 38, ll. 1–16 (Mr. P teaching Mary)
3. Junior apologizes to Mr. P:
   "I'm sorry about your face" (p. 34, l. 16)
   Mr. P apologizes to Junior:
   - for him having been suspended (p. 35, l. 1)
   - for the way the Indians have been treated by (white) teachers in school (p. 37, ll. 1 f.)
   - for the way Indians have been treated in general ("We were trying to kill Indian culture", p. 37, l. 4)
4. The narrator's family react in a way typical of people used to bowing to authority: one of their number has been punished, so they all think he must have deserved it. They are disappointed in him (p. 34, l. 10). His act was spontaneous, and uncharacteristically aggressive, but he probably hoped his family would at least sympathise a little with his frustration. Students might understand these reactions, or find them exaggerated and unfair.
5. Character profile of Mary Runs Away:
   - Junior's big sister (p. 28, ll. 17/18)
   - graduated from high school and then stopped fulfilling expectations: no college, no job ("my sister just froze", p. 28, ll. 25/26)
   - "beautiful, strong and funny" (p. 28, ll. 26/27)
   - Mr. P knows that she wanted to write romance novels (p. 38, ll. 10 ff.)
   - says she was even smarter than Junior (p. 38, l. 3)
   - was always writing stories while still at school, but never dared to show them to anyone but Mr. P (p. 40, ll. 3 ff.)

   - is presumed to be depressed (p. 41, l. 7)
6. Rowdy (cf. unit 1, ch. 3) new info here from Mr. P:
   - he will just get "meaner and meaner" (p. 42, l. 21)
   - he is one of those people who have given up hope and hurts others because he wants them to feel as bad as he does (p. 43, ll. 10–22)
   - he protects Junior because he is "the only good thing in his life. He doesn't want to give that up." (p. 43, ll. 13/14)

Chapters 6/7 (Leaving Wellpinit High School)
➤ **Copymaster 7**
Possible answers:

1. a) Alternatives to Wellpinit High School:
   - Hunters, "on the west end of the reservation, filled with poor Indians and poorer white kids" (p. 46, ll. 14/15)
   - Springdale, "a school on the reservation border filled with the poorest Indians and poorer-than-poorest white kids" (p. 46, ll. 19/20)

   Neither of these is a viable choice because standards at these schools are worse than in Wellpinit.
   - Reardan, "a rich white farm town … 22 miles away from the rez … filled with farmers and rednecks and racist cops" (p. 46, ll. 24 ff.), with "one of the best small schools in the state" (p. 46, l. 30)

   Going to Reardan initially seems an impossible goal to Junior ("it seemed as real as saying, 'I want to fly to the moon.'", "going to Reardan is truly a strange idea", p. 47, l. 2, l. 16). Nevertheless it is the only reasonable choice of school for him, even though he is told that it will be hard for him to get there and back every day (p. 47, ll. 22 f.), and that his fellow tribal members will hate him (p. 47, ll. 27 ff.).

   b) At first Rowdy doesn't want to believe the news but when he realizes that it's the truth he screams out in anger and pain. He absolutely refuses to even consider joining his friend at Reardan, because he hates everything the school stands for; instead, Rowdy punches Junior in the face, thereby making it clear that he has turned from best friend into worst enemy.
2. (Extra) Possible qualities to be valued in friendship: trust, kindness, sympathy, humour, liveliness, understanding, tolerance, helpfulness, encouragement, loyalty, common interests …

   Possible definition of friendship: Friendship is a relationship between people who know each other well, and who can trust each other in all kinds of situations. They support or help each other in need, and they enjoy talking, laughing and spending time together. (Personal statements will vary and focus on different elements.)

NOTE   After reading the chapters, choose a few of the tasks below to do either individually, in pairs or in a group. At least one of them should involve writing so that you can put it in your reading journal.

TASKS   1   Read chapters 4 and 5. Tell each other what happens and why.

2   Talk about what you found surprising/sad/funny/interesting/unexpected about these chapters. Choose a short passage which illustrates this impression and read it out loud to your partner/group.

3   In chapter 5: Who apologizes to whom and for what? Write a comment for your reading journal.

4   Can you understand why the narrator's family react to his suspension in this way? Do you agree with their reaction? Write a short statement and put it in your reading journal.

5   For your reading journal, start a character profile of Mary, the narrator's sister.

6   Alternatively, concentrate on Rowdy and add new information to the profile you began after reading chapter 3.

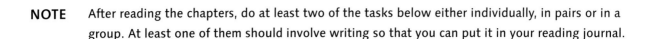
NOTE   After reading the chapters, do at least two of the tasks below either individually, in pairs or in a group. At least one of them should involve writing so that you can put it in your reading journal.

TASKS   **1**   Read chapters 6 and 7. Focus on the following questions:

a) What are the narrator's alternatives to Wellpinit High School, and how reasonable are they?

b) How does Rowdy take the news of his friend's decision to go to a different school?

2   **(Extra)** Reflecting your personal attitude to friendship
- Make a list of all your friends.
- Make a list of qualities that you particularly value in friendships. Match the two lists to show which of your friends has which particular qualities.
- Define friendship and make a personal statement on its importance for you.
- You might want to add an illustration of your own (cf. cartoon p. 94).

End of Unit 2

TASKS   **1**   Write the unit summary.

2   Before you go on reading unit 3, think about what it means in general to go to a new school. List a few things, perhaps even from your own experience.

3   What specific problems will the narrator be faced with when transferring from Wellpinit to Reardan High School? Make five different statements using the following words or phrases:

> he might – maybe – he will probably – perhaps – it could be that –
> it is very likely that – he is likely to – I can imagine that – no doubt

End of Unit 2 ➤ Copymaster 7

Possible answers:

1. cf. summary on p. 18
2. being alone, feeling like an outsider, the chance to meet new people, to start 'from scratch', having to make new friends (even if you are shy), finding your way around an unknown place, having to ask a lot of questions, having to give a lot of information about yourself, …
3. It is very likely that he won't find friends in the new school easily.
   It could be that he will have problems following the lessons there.

I can imagine that the white students will mock him because of his physical handicaps.
Maybe/Perhaps he can quickly join the basketball team and get to know some of his team mates faster and better.
He will probably have difficulties getting to school on time.
He might have to give up because of the 22-mile distance between the school and the rez.

Unit 3 (pp. 53–90): An Outsider in Reardan

Summary

Junior – known at Reardan High by his "real" name Arnold Spirit – has a difficult time settling in at his new school while still remaining a resident of the rez. The kids at Reardan are more or less openly racist and call Junior insulting names, so that eventually Junior hits his main aggressor, Roger, in the face. When Roger does not fight back, Junior realizes that the "rules of fisticuffs" apparently do not apply everywhere. After talking to his grandmother, Junior learns that Roger has now begun to respect him, especially after he sees Junior on his father's friend's vintage motorbike. However, the most popular girl in his class, Penelope, still does not pay him much attention, although she does let him join her in a Halloween fund-raising activity for homeless people and shows sympathy when Arnold is robbed of his earnings by some fellow Indians.

Note: Junior states that since the Reardan mascot was an Indian, he "was the only other Indian in town" (p. 54, ll. 33/34, cf. cartoon on p. 55). Immediately after mentioning this mascot, the narrator speaks of "racist Reardan" (p. 55, l. 1).

Students might want to discuss the mascot issue on the basis of the following information.

> **Mascots**
>
> For almost a century now, white American schools have been using names for their sports teams which allude to Native American culture such as "Redskins" or "Braves", as well as mascots depicting Indian chiefs, or Indian sacred objects (e. g. special feathers or drums or articles of clothing). These mascots, however, are often understood by Natives to have racist undertones instead of actually honouring the Native culture, as some people claim they

do. As C. Pewewardy from the University of Kansas writes, "Teachers should research the matter and discover that American Indians would never have associated the sacred practices of becoming a warrior with the hoopla of a high school pep rally, brave and princess pageantry, half-time entertainment, or being a sidekick to cheerleaders."

> (From: www.racismagainstindians.org/STARArticle/
> IndianImagery.htm)

Since the late 1970s and in the wake of political correctness, there have been many attempts to ban such mascots from schools. Opponents of the tradition claim that it would not be permitted to use any other ethnic group as a mascot, e. g. there would never be a team called "The Negroes" or "The Asians". Why then, they ask, is "The Sioux" or any other tribal Indian name acceptable? As a result, many team names and mascots have indeed been changed. However there is also a lot of emotional opposition to this because for decades people have identified with the old team names.

Websites:
www.mascotdb.com
www.dmoz.org/Sports/Team_Spirit/Mascots

Chapters 8–10 (Coping) ➤ Copymaster 8

Possible answers:

1. "Those kids weren't just white. They were translucent." (p. 54, l. 24); "more than half of every graduating class went to college" (p. 55, ll. 1/2); cartoon on p. 56; a blond girl named "Penelope" (p. 57, l. 19, p. 58, l. 1); name "Junior" considered odd (p. 58, ll. 15 ff.), "they followed a whole other set of mysterious rules" (p. 63, l. 22)
2. a) On the rez, the narrator is known as "Junior" (along with many other Indians across the USA, apparently), so he has never felt there was anything unusual about it.

NOTE　Choose a few tasks from the following to discuss with a partner and/or in class. If there is writing involved, include your answers in your reading journal.

TASKS

1　"Reardan was the opposite of the rez." (p. 55, l. 4): Find as many passages as possible from chapter 8 to explain how the narrator means this.

2　What's in a name?
  a) Discuss the situation in the classroom described on page 59. Comment on the narrator's, the teacher's and the other pupils' attitude to what his "real name" is.
  b) Re-read the insulting names that Junior is called by those who bully him on his way home (p. 61). Research and discuss what makes these names so insulting.
  c) Comment on Roger's "joke" (p. 62) that leads to Junior punching him.

3　Written and unwritten rules: Comment on how they influence not only Junior's, but any teenager's life (pp. 59 f., p. 63).

4　"I think it means he respects you" (p. 66, l. 16): Explain Grandma's interpretation of Roger's behaviour with regard to the following encounter between Roger and Arnold (p. 68, l. 24 – p. 69, l. 5).

5　Comment on Penelope's rejection of Arnold (p. 69) in the light of Roger's newly found respect for him.

6　Collect information on a) Grandma and b) Eugene and write a short profile of one of them. Remember to update your profile as you proceed through the novel.

7　a) Discuss the title of chapter 10, "Tears of a Clown".
  b) What do you think is the function of the chapter at this stage of the story?

He cannot understand why both the class and the teacher at Reardan laugh at this. Here, he must go by his "real name", i. e. his official name "Arnold Spirit", which nobody at home ever uses.

b) "Chief", "Tonto", "Squaw Boy", "Redskin" and "Sitting Bull" (p. 61, l. 10 and cartoon) all allude to white clichés of Indians.
- "Tonto" means "stupid" in Spanish
- "Squaw" means a female Indian
- "Sitting Bull" is the name of a warrior chief in the Indian Wars, and as such is also the embodiment of a cliché – the Indian warrior, potential killer.
- "Redskin" reduces a Native Indian to the colour of his or her skin (cf. "Red Indian"); sometimes the word is also seen to refer to the bloody skins of Natives who were scalped after a battle.

c) The "joke" (p. 62, ll. 20/21) is racist in several points: it uses the taboo term "niggers", it implies that black people behave like animals, and claims that Indians are the product of this subhuman behaviour.

3. In any teenager's life, there are (mostly unwritten) rules defining how to dress, how to speak and how to behave in order to be popular or at least accepted within the peer group. The "rules of fisticuffs" (pp. 59/60) have always been tough on Junior, because he inevitably ends up getting beaten up. And yet he has always adhered to them because they are the accepted social code in the reservation. When Roger does not respect these rules, Junior is completely confused and asks him about the rules of fighting at Reardan. Roger responds in puzzlement: "What rules?", (p. 63, l. 27), and Junior thus learns that at Reardan these rules do not seem to exist.

4. Grandma says that because Junior was brave enough to attack the alpha male, that male now respects him. The same applies to rest of the "pack". When Arnold arrives at school on Eugene's motorbike, Roger's respect for him seems to increase, since now he is not only the brave attacker, but also someone to be envied for riding on a vintage motorbike.

5. Penelope seems to have nothing but contempt for the male craze for fighting and motorbikes. Arnold's attempt at fighting the "alpha male" is for her simply an example of typical male behaviour and she thoroughly fails to see the point of it.

6. a) Grandma (see cartoon p. 65):
She dresses simply and cheaply, uses her deceased husband's belt, wears different-coloured bandannas depending on the occasion, makes a delicious salmon dish, creates typical Aboriginal key-chains to sell on eBay (by pretending they are "highly sacred" charms she cleverly exploits people's desire for exotic ethnic objects). Junior loves and admires her for being "the smartest person on the planet" (p. 69, l. 7)

b) Eugene (see cartoon p. 67):
Dad's best friend; "a good guy" (p. 67, l. 10), "drunk all the time" (l. 11) but good-humoured (p. 68, ll. 1 ff.); wears long braids (p. 68, l. 9); praises Junior for going to Reardan ("It's pretty cool, you doing this", l. 16); regards himself as a "wuss" (l. 18)

7. a) The title of the chapter refers to Junior's emotional outburst when Rowdy tells him about Dawn's indifference towards him, and how Junior now realizes that he "was quite a dramatic twelve-year-old" (p. 68, l. 17). Clowns are supposed to make others laugh by making fools of themselves. They are not, however, meant to be taken seriously or to take themselves seriously.

b) The chapter is a flashback to when Junior and Rowdy were 12, and Junior was in love with a girl called Dawn. Rowdy called him stupid, but kept his secret because he was his best friend. Both of these things are parallels to Junior's "new life": Again he is in love with a girl who obviously "doesn't give a shit about" him (p. 71, l. 10) but this time he cannot talk to Rowdy about it, because he no longer considers himself to be Junior's best friend. Junior misses his "secret-keeper" (p. 71, l. 27) at least as much as he longs for Penelope's attention.

Chapters 11/12 (Settling In) ➤ Copymaster 9
Possible answers:

1. (Extra) Celebrated on the last day of October; the name comes from "All Hallows' Eve" because 1st of November is traditionally All Saints', or "All Hallows'" day. Children and young teenagers dress up in fancy or scary costumes, have parties and go "trick-or-treating", mainly collecting sweets or money. Some youngsters also collect money or food for needy people (cf. Penelope's plan).
Symbols of Halloween include witches, black cats, skeletons and pumpkins with faces carved into them out of which the light of a candle shines; these lanterns are called "jack-o'-lanterns" in memory of an old (Irish) story about "Jack" who after his death had to wander the earth with his lantern because neither heaven nor hell wanted him. (cf. http://usa.usembassy.de/holidays-halloween.htm)

2. (Extra) a) On Halloween (or Carnival) people tend to dress up in something different from their usual dress in order to have fun and switch identities for a while: e. g. girls like to dress up as princesses or witches, boys as pirates or cowboys, etc. There is also an element of competition in it (whose costume is the scariest/prettiest/most striking/most daring).

b) Penelope has chosen the costume of a "homeless woman" for two reasons, one of which she is possibly not aware of. On the one hand, the costume is a "political statement" (p. 73, l. 2). But it also symbolizes the exact opposite of what she is like in real life,

NOTE After reading the chapters, choose a few of the following tasks to do individually, in pairs or in small groups. Choose at least one task that involves writing and include the results in your reading journal.

TASKS 1 **(Extra)** Do some research on Halloween and its importance in American communities. Give a short presentation in class including special vocabulary.

2 **(Extra)** Wearing a costume
   a) Why do people choose certain costumes for themselves (e. g. on Halloween in the USA, during "Karneval", "Fasching" or "Fastnacht" in Germany)? What do costumes express? Discuss.
   b) Comment on Penelope's and Arnold's "homeless dude" / "homeless woman" costumes (p. 72, ll. 1, 4). Why are they wearing them? And what is the effect on each other?

3 Junior uses vivid imagery when describing his feelings during and after the attack on him on Halloween (p. 74, ll. 3–5). What does it make you imagine? Draw a cartoon like those Junior draws, and explain it to your partner or class.

4 Loneliness: On the basis of pp. 76–80 (l. 10) explain and comment on Junior's feelings concerning the rez and Reardan. Include a detailed explanation of the following sentences in your commentary: "He walked away. I stood there and waited for the rocks to replace my bones and blood." (p. 80, ll. 9–10). Also consider the cartoon on page 79.

5 **(Extra)** Read the episode of the science lesson on petrified wood out loud in small groups, taking turns reading. Then turn it into a short sketch to act out in class, including the short encounter between Junior and Gordy after the lesson (p. 80, ll. 3–10).

6 What about Penelope's point of view? Write a diary entry for Penelope on the evening of the science lesson described on pp. 77–79.

7 Marrying a stranger
   a) Mary's marriage to a Flathead Indian in Montana worries her family. Explain why.
   b) Discuss why such a situation might generally worry a family, i. e. if their daughter/sister or son/brother ran away to live with a complete stranger.

8 **(Extra)** What are the theoretical and practical conclusions that Junior draws from his sister's marriage (p. 84, ll. 3–20)? Write a comment. You might even want to put some of his ideas in a cartoon.

9 Friendship
   a) Identify the steps in the development of the friendship between Arnold and Gordy.
   b) Compare this friendship with the one between Junior and Rowdy on the rez. Write a short paragraph to include in your reading journal.

10 The joys of reading and studying: Discuss the advice Gordy gives Arnold (pp. 86–90) with a partner, and compare it to your personal attitude towards reading. Write a short statement to include in your reading journal.

11 Getting to and from school
   a) Look at the cartoon on p. 81, and the description on p. 80, ll. 11–31. What does this tell you about Junior's determination to go to Reardan considering his family's poverty?
   b) Can you imagine doing the same thing for education (or anything else of similar importance for you personally)? Write a short statement to include in your reading journal.

End of Unit 3

TASKS   1 Write the unit summary.

2 Discuss Junior's situation at Reardan at this point (end of chapter 12), and make two lists concerning:
   – improvements in Junior's situation so far
   – what he still needs in order to improve his situation further

3 Choose one of the chapters in unit 3 and explain its title.

something which is made clearer in chapter 15, p. 99, ll. 12 ff. Nevertheless, the effect on Arnold is that she looks "beautiful" and "cute" (p. 72, ll. 5, 14). In his opinion, Arnold has not really changed his appearance, as he usually looks "half-homeless anyway" (p. 72, l. 3). However, Penelope sees it as a "good costume" that makes Junior look "really homeless". She is not aware of the irony of this, because she has no idea of Arnold's poverty.

3. Imagery describing Junior's feelings:
   – "the spit made me feel like an insect" (p. 74, l. 3): An insect is usually considered a worthless creature, small, often a pest, easily crushed or killed.
   – "Like a slug burning to death from salty spit." (l. 5): A slug is larger than an insect, but more disgusting. They're slimy and gardeners often kill them by pouring salt on them.
   – The cartoon could show a slug being hit by a giant blob of spit or being burnt by salt.

4. Junior is lonely on the rez because his former friends have turned their backs on him. He is even lonelier in Reardan because everybody just ignores him ("Roger … didn't socialise with me" p. 77, ll. 9/10; "I just walked … alone, I sat at lunch alone … and played catch with myself", ll. 12/13). He uses his journey to school every day as a metaphor for the change taking place within himself: "somewhere on the road to Reardan, I became something less than an Indian" (ll. 3/4). Even his teacher ignores him, and refuses to believe what he says. However when the class genius, Gordy, corroborates Junior's point, Gordy is thanked for his valuable contribution to the lesson and Junior is not even acknowledged by the teacher. (p. 79, ll. 1 ff.). Arnold's feeling of solitude and loneliness is made worse when Gordy does not accept his thanks and says he did not do it for Junior but for science. This is when the narrator says "I waited for the rocks to replace my bones and blood" (p. 80, ll. 9 f.). The image is taken from the science lesson, in which students learned that rocks actually replace wood when it becomes petrified. Arnold uses it to mean that the extent of indifference towards him as a person is petrifying him, i. e. turning him from a living being into a lifeless piece of rock.

5. (Extra) Individual answers

6. "A funny thing happened in the science lesson today. Arnold, the new Indian kid who never says anything in class, actually raised his hand to contradict Mr. Dodge! We couldn't believe it! I've never talked back to a teacher in my life! Dodge let him have his say, all about how petrified wood isn't wood at all (how much sense does that make?) … but he was actually really angry and said that if that information came from the reservation it couldn't really be true, could it, and I think we all thought the same. But then the class whiz-kid, Gordy,

stood up and said Arnold was right! I guess even Dodge knows that when Gordy says something it's probably true, so maybe this Arnold guy isn't as stupid as he looks, even with a face full of zits. I wonder …"

7. a) Mary's family are used to the whole family sticking close by one another and not moving away ("We Spirits stay in one place", p. 82, l. 12). They are probably also worried because he's a gambler (l. 25), he's ugly (l. 33) and in Junior's opinion the Indians in Montana are dangerous (p. 83, ll. 6 ff.).
   b) Most families would probably be worried if their daughter or son ran away to marry someone they didn't even know and live far away from the rest of the family. They wouldn't know when they would see her or him again, and they might worry that she or he had fallen for a bad person who would turn out to be dangerous. The same worries apply to Mary and her family.

8. (Extra) Junior realizes that Mary has taken the first opportunity she was offered to fulfil her romantic dreams ("And then I realized that my sister was trying to LIVE a romance novel." p. 83, ll. 14/15) because as he sees it, her spirit was not killed while she was "underground" (in the basement) watching TV and doing nothing after all. He compares her running away to his own situation, and decides they are both warriors who are not afraid of confrontations. As a result of coming to this conclusion about himself, he confronts Gordy the next day and thus begins their strange friendship.

9. a) Arnold takes the initiative and talks to Gordy. They get into a discussion about computers (in which Arnold feels incompetent and Gordy feels the need to teach him some difficult words). Gordy realizes that although Arnold may not know those words, he has "a singular wit" (p. 85, ll. 27 f.). Arnold comes straight to the point and tells Gordy that he wants to be his friend. Gordy eventually becomes interested in Arnold, and the two start studying together.
   b) Arnold/Junior explains that his friendship with Gordy is different from the one with Rowdy because with Gordy he cannot share secrets or dreams (p. 86, ll. 27/28). However, Gordy can teach him things in the library or the computer room. Arnold wants to be his friend because they are both weird and different from the others, and they are both intellectual (ll. 22 ff.).
   Rowdy was born on the same day as Junior and the two were always the "best of friends" (l. 27). Rowdy is violent and non-intellectual, but before Junior betrayed him (as he sees it) by going to Reardan, he had never been violent towards Junior and rather protected him from the bullies on the rez. The two boys shared all their secrets and dreams with one another.

10. Important points to note and discuss:
    - "read a book three times" (p. 86, ll. 32/33): for its plot, for the history and words, for the mystery of life (However, Gordy never explicitly says what he expects from the third reading.)
    - novels, and the words used in them, should be taken seriously (ll. 18/19)
    - books are mysteries that teach you how much more you need to learn (p. 89, ll. 21/22)
    - really good books give you joy ("a metaphorical boner", p. 89, l. 30)

11. a) It is such a hardship for Junior that it can be called a sacrifice he makes for education: He often has to walk at least part of the 22 miles (one way) before he can hitch a ride, and he gets "blisters each time" (p. 80, l. 31). Nevertheless he accepts this because he feels that getting an education at Reardan is the only way he can ever fulfil his dream of having a better life than that on the rez.

    b) Individual answers

End of Unit 3 ➤ Copymaster 9
Possible answers:
1. cf. summary on p. 21
2. Improvements in Junior's situation at Reardan:
   - he is no longer bullied
   - he has a friend who studies with him
   - he has become used to the situation between rez and Reardan (getting to and from school)
   - he has found out that he is more intelligent than most of the other students (p. 77, l. 20)

   What he still needs to improve his situation further:
   - apart from Gordy he still has no friends
   - Penelope still ignores him
   - his teachers still do not respect him
3. "How to Fight Monsters":
   In this chapter, Junior learns that his one act of punching Roger (who represents the monsters worrying him all the time) was enough to gain Roger's respect – and that all he had learned about fighting on the reservation does not apply at Reardan.

   "Slouching Toward Thanksgiving":
   Slouching means moving in a lazy and undetermined way, which reflects the narrator's "zombie"-like existence at Reardan ("I walked like a zombie through the next few weeks in Reardan", p. 76, l. 1).

Unit 4 (pp. 91–122): Gradual Acceptance in Reardan

Summary
Around Thanksgiving, while Rowdy is still furious with his one-time best friend, Junior manages to make some friends at Reardan. He falls in love with Penelope, and she allows him to be her boyfriend, even when she learns of his poverty.

Chapters 13/14 (Family And Friends on the Rez) ➤ Copymaster 10
Possible answers:
1. Mary is very enthusiastic and positive about her new life ("I love it here" p. 91, l. 7, "It was a dream come true! I love my life!" p. 92, pp. 23/24); she experienced new things ("I rode a horse for the first time", p. 91, l. 8); loved her honeymoon at a hotel ("the best part" p. 92, l. 6); lives on a very different kind of reservation in Montana which is bigger ("a lot of towns for one rez" p. 91, l. 14), where Indians and white people live together (p. 91, ll. 15/16), where Indians have a more traditional way of life ("Indians still ride horses in Montana" p. 91, ll. 8/9), but she doesn't manage to find a job despite sending off many applications (p. 91, ll. 9/10).

2. (Extra) M(ary): Hi, Junior; it's me, your sister!
   J(unior): Sis! Nice to hear from you; how's life going?
   M: Beautiful, I just love it here in Montana. Can you believe it – I rode a horse for the first time in my life!
   J: But are you really getting on there alright? Aren't the Montana Indians strange? Are they treating you ok?
   M: Yeah well, it's very different to Wellpinit here. You know, there are over twenty restaurants on this rez. Just imagine that!
   J: Hm, and what do you do all day when you're not riding horses? (ha ha)
   M: Well, I've been sending out applications to all these restaurants, but no luck so far; I'm still looking for a job. But, listen, have I told you about our honeymoon trip yet? …

NOTE   Choose from the following tasks and activities. Some of the tasks can be done as a continuation of tasks you have already dealt with in connection with former chapters. In these cases, it would make sense to choose these over other tasks which deal with completely new issues. Compare your notes and reading journals with other students.

TASKS   1   Continue your profile of Junior's sister Mary after reading her e-mail.

2   **(Extra)** With a partner, turn Mary's e-mail into a telephone conversation and act it out to the class. Make sure you add plausible comments from Junior based on what you know of his feelings for her and his attitude towards her marriage.

3   **(Extra)** Thanksgiving
   a)   Do some research into the meaning and importance of the holiday for Americans and give a presentation in class.
   b)   "I always think it's funny when Indians celebrate Thanksgiving" (p. 93, l. 5). Explain Junior's comment on the basis of all you know about Thanksgiving, and of what the narrator tells us (p. 93). Write a short paragraph for your reading journal.

4   Respect and friendship
   a)   With a partner, talk about what you understand of the episode with Rowdy and the cartoon (p. 93, l. 14 – p. 95, l. 15).
   b)   Then write a short comment on Junior's feelings described on p. 95, ll. 9–15 for your reading journal.

3. (Extra) a)

Thanksgiving or Thanksgiving Day
is celebrated as a federal holiday in the USA on the fourth Thursday in November every year. On this day, people celebrate by getting together with family or friends for a holiday feast. Typically, a big meal is served consisting of roasted turkey with stuffing, cranberry sauce, mashed potatoes and gravy, as well other autumn vegetables such as sweet potatoes, sweet corn, and pumpkin pie. Thanksgiving stems from the time when the first settlers in America wanted to give a communal thanks to God for having brought them safely to the New World, and also to thank the Indians for helping them grow crops in order to survive. It is usual to start a Thanksgiving dinner by saying grace. During this time of year, people often help those members of the community who cannot afford their own meal by donating money or organizing gifts of food.

b) As Junior says, in the beginning, the first Settlers in America and the Indians were friends, but later on they became worst enemies (p. 93, ll. 6 ff.). The Natives felt deceived by the American settlers and a lot of Indians were killed, their land was taken from them and their lifestyle changed considerably as a result.
Considering this background, Junior finds it understandably strange that this very white American holiday should also be an important day of feasting for the descendants of the victims of the American settlers.

4. a) Junior remembers that it was a sort of 'tradition' between him and his best friend Rowdy to have a "pumpkin pie eating contest" (p. 93, ll. 15/16). Remembering that makes him really miss his friend. He draws a cartoon for Rowdy in which he depicts "the way we used to be" (p. 94, l. 1) to show Rowdy how much he misses their friendship. Rowdy's father reacts without respect or understanding for this act of friendship and calls Junior "gay" (p. 94, l. 11).

b) Junior takes some consolation from the fact that Rowdy looks sad and does not tear up the cartoon. Junior interprets this as a sign of Rowdy's respect for his cartoons and maybe for himself, too.

Chapters 15/16 (Penelope) ➤ Copymaster 11
Note: On page 97, ll. 3-6, there is a reference to Mahatma Gandhi's apparent obsession with his bowel movements. However, this was not, as Arnold Spirit speculates, a way of defining "the condition and quality of his life", but rather, as historians note, a preoccupation with his health, since regular bowel movements are considered healthy.

(From: http://www.thaindian.com/newsportal/india-news/ mahatma-gandhis-toilet-shifted-back-to-sabarmati- museum_10095210.html)

Possible answers:
1. a) "anorexia" (OALD): an emotional disorder, especially affecting young women, in which there is an abnormal fear of becoming fat, causing the person to stop eating and leading to dangerous weight loss.
"bulimia" (OALD): an emotional disorder in which a person repeatedly eats too much and then forces him- or herself to vomit.

Eating Disorders: Anorexia and Bulimia
Anorexia nervosa and *bulimia nervosa* (usually just called "anorexia" and "bulimia") are the most common types of eating disorder.
Anorexic people are unnaturally afraid of gaining weight, and they usually believe they are too fat, even if in reality they are very thin. They restrict their food intake and often tend to do excessive amounts of physical exercise.
Bulimia is similar to anorexia, except that a bulimic person does eat – sometimes excessive amounts of high-calorie food, such as so-called junk food, and sometimes in secret – and then tries to compensate for this binge by forcing him- or herself to vomit or by doing excessive physical exercise in order to prevent weight gain.
While an anorexic person becomes very thin and is usually underweight, a person with bulimia may be of a normal weight, or even overweight.

(From: http://kidshealth.org/teen/food_fitness/problems/ eat_disorder.html)

b) Penelope's eating disorder bulimia (OALD) is an emotional disorder in which a person repeatedly eats too much and then forces him- or herself to vomit. Penelope calls herself "bulimic" and is insistent that she is not "anorexic" (p. 98, l. 21). She thinks that she has her eating disorder under control, because she can decide when and where she is sick (p. 98, ll. 29/30).
She covers up the smell of vomit by chewing gum. When Junior expresses his sympathy ("Don't give up" p. 99, l. 9) she admits her fears and worries to him, which she believes nobody understands or even suspects because from the outside, her life seems to be perfect.

2. (Extra) a) **Note**: Gordy is inclined to see the scientific side of things and uses technical vocabulary. This should be reflected in students' dialogues.
A(rnold): Gordy, what do you know about bulimia?
G(ordy): Ah, you mean 'bulimia nervosa'? I came across that once when I was googling 'anorexia nervosa' after reading about it in a book.
A: Yeah, well, so you know the difference between the two?

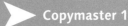

NOTE   After reading the chapters, choose a few of the following tasks to do individually, in pairs or in small groups. Make sure you also do some writing for your reading journal.

TASKS   1   Anorexic or bulimic?
   a) Look up *anorexia* and *bulimia* (cf. p. 98, l. 21) in a monolingual dictionary, and if you like, add some research on these disorders.
   b) Explain Penelope's eating disorder and the way she deals with it in a matter-of-fact way.

2   **(Extra)** Imagine one of the following scenarios and write a short dialogue. Consider the register that the characters involved would use.
   a) Arnold speaks to Gordy about bulimia without mentioning Penelope.
   b) Junior tells his parents about his experience in the school bathroom.
   Act out your dialogues in class.

3   Being "the hot item at Reardan High School" (p. 100, ll. 6/7): Explain how you understand the relationship of Penelope and Junior.

4   **(Extra)** Write a diary entry for Penelope on her feelings concerning Arnold Spirit.

5   From what you know about the two, list arguments for and against Arnold and Penelope having a relationship.

6   Being popular
   a) Penelope knows that "she's pretty and smart and popular" (p. 99, ll. 12–15). Explain what "being popular" means for a student like Penelope at high school.
   b) Discuss to what extent Arnold Spirit actually shares her popularity (cf. p. 101, l. 22: "After all, I suddenly became popular.").

7   **(Extra)** Study the description Junior gives of Penelope playing volleyball (pp. 106–107) and comment on the images he uses (esp. p. 106, ll. 6–9). What do they tell you about how he sees the relationship? Write a short paragraph for your reading journal.

8   Is Junior a racist? Discuss Junior's being in love with Penelope on the background of Rowdy's and Gordy's comments (p. 107, ll. 20/21 + p. 108). Also take Junior's own comments into consideration (p. 100, ll. 9–12 + p. 101, ll. 14–21 + pp. 102–104). Write a short statement to put in your reading journal.

G: A person with anorexia goes on an extreme diet and still thinks she – or occasionally he, I guess – is too fat when in reality they might be stick thin; thin enough not to survive which, as I understand it, they sometimes don't! A person with bulimia, on the other hand, often gorges herself or himself on junk food and then goes to the bathroom to vomit, so the calories won't make them gain weight.

A: But heck, why do they do it?? …

b) **Note**: This is a situation in which Junior can say what he thinks and feels, but because he is talking to adults he will probably use fairly neutral (and definitely not technical) vocabulary.

J(unior): Mom, Dad, I have to tell you about a really special girl in Reardan.

Dad: Go on, son, who is she?

J: Her name is Penelope and she's incredible.

Mom: So are you, Junior!

J: Alright Mom! Anyway, Penelope doesn't seem to believe that about herself. She's really popular and pretty but guess what I caught her doing today?

Mom: Tell us, Junior!

J: Well, I was in the bathroom when I heard these awful vomiting noises coming from the girls' bathroom, and I thought maybe somebody was really sick, you know? So I waited for them to come out, and then Penelope came out chewing cinnamon gum, but I could still smell the vomit on her breath. And when I called her anorexic, she started acting really proud, saying she was actually bulimic, and all that.

Dad: You see, son, everybody has their problems.

J: Yeah, sure – but heck, she's so …

3. Individual answers

4. (Extra) (possible beginning) "Today this weird guy Arnold Spirit caught me throwing up in the girls' bathroom, and he had the nerve to stand there staring at me when I came out. But actually he seems like an alright guy, at least he listened to me when …"

5. For: they are both clever (p. 38, l. 3, p. 99, l. 14), seem to fancy each other (p. 102, ll. 1 ff.), like being together (p. 100, ll. 6 ff.), and don't seem to care what others think about their relationship, also seem to trust and talk to each other about their dreams (p. 102, ll. 20 ff.)
Against: they are from completely different backgrounds, Penelope's father is a racist (p. 100, l. 13); the two lead very different lives, money could turn into a serious problem because Arnold wouldn't be able to take Penelope out as much as she wanted.

6. a) good-looking, clever/intelligent, liked and accepted by classmates, successful in the classroom and out of it (i.e. sports), self-confident, interested in others and interesting to others …
b) Penelope is courageous enough to go against her father's idea of what a 'suitable' boyfriend is (p. 100,

ll. 14 ff.); being with Penelope increases Arnold's popularity: he is interesting enough for a 'popular' girl because he's 'different' (Indian, poor, an outsider), so it seems that being different helps Arnold become popular; he is close to Penelope because they share her secret (her bulimia and its causes) as well as their "big dreams". (p. 103, ll. 16–18)

7. (Extra) Arnold admires Penelope ("a work of art", p. 106, l. 3); he sees her as a completely "white" person, skin and clothes ("she was all white on white on white", l. 7) which he finds enormously attractive and desirable ("I want to be her chocolate topping", l. 9); he calls her skin "pale white", which is a tautology (cf. Gordy's definition p. 85, l. 16), then he conjures up images of "milk" and "clouds" to compare to her whiteness. Finally, he compares the complete impression of her to a dessert, i. e. a vanilla cake.
Note: Here he is probably thinking of a typically American vanilla-flavoured cake called "Angel food cake", baked using only the whites of eggs, which makes it very pale in colour.
He wants to "be her chocolate topping" (p. 106, l. 9), which means he wants to be an integral part of the dessert, and is aware of the contrast in colours: the topping is equally sweet and completes the cake (maybe even with a sexual implication).

8. Rowdy writes that white women are "like bowling trophies" for Indian guys (p. 107, l. 21). He obviously believes that Penelope's main attraction for Junior is that she is white, and that it would be a triumph for him if he could make out with her.
Gordy does some seemingly absurd research, focuses on "white girl" without seeing any real context.
The outcome of both, nevertheless, is the same.
Arnold/Junior: "I'm an Indian boy… How can I get a white girl to love me?" (p. 107, ll. 24 f.): This comment shows that Arnold does think in terms of race and that he is aware of the gap between Indians and whites concerning hope and opportunities, so this way of thinking is normal for him. His interpretation of their relationship "And I was the smudge" (pp. 100–102, esp. p. 101, l. 20) shows that he is actually exploiting the racist aspect of their relationship ("I was kind of using her, too", p. 101, l. 21). However, he also distinguishes between the shallow reasons for their relationship and the "bigger and better reasons" (p. 102, ll. 18 f.), which are their common dreams of making better lives for themselves. When he mentions those, he puts Penelope and himself on the same level (p. 103, ll. 16–21).

Chapters 17/18 (Friends) ▶ Copymaster 12
Possible answers:

1. a) cf. chapter 2

b) The strategy of pretence:
   - he lies (p. 109, l. 15, p. 111, ll. 24 ff., p. 113, ll. 18/19, p. 116, l. 23, p. 117, ll. 5/6, 14)
   - he pretends not to be hungry at lunch time, to suffer from illness or physical handicap, to be a disbeliever in modern technology like an i-Pod or to have obligations on the rez (cartoon)
   - he pretends to be middle class and to have money (p. 109, ll. 13/14; p. 110, ll. 12/13)

   The strategy of avoidance:
   - he avoids situations in which it might be obvious that he hasn't got any money/is poor ("meet P. at the gym for the dance", p. 111, l. 26; "I'd wait in the parking lot until everybody was gone", p. 113, l. 25)
   - he keeps quiet ("I'd made it through the evening without revealing my poverty", p. 113, l. 20, "I was completely relieved that we'd forgotten", l. 17)

   c)
   - Penelope is delighted with Arnold's outfit (= his Dad's old suit) calling it "retroactive" and "radioactive" (p. 112, ll. 16/17).
   - Penelope realizes they forgot their photo.
   - Roger, not Arnold, persuades Penelope's father to let her go.
   - Arnold orders food although he knows he cannot pay for it, goes to the bathroom and pretends unsuccessfully to be sick.
   - Roger talks to him about joining the basketball team etc., he acts very "nice" and "polite" (p. 116, l. 14)
   - Arnold tells him he forgot his wallet, Roger immediately offers to lend him forty dollars.
   - Roger takes Arnold and Penelope back to the school.
   - Arnold tells them his father will pick him up there.
   - Penelope has heard from Roger that he lent Arnold money. She asks Arnold if he's poor.
   - Arnold admits to it.

   d) In the cartoon, Arnold depicts various answers he would have liked to have given instead of the one he did give ("no" and finally, "yes"), because they would have made him look either "cool" ("no"), witty ("pores"), clever ("poverty is a relative thing" …) or shocked ("gasp"). In the real situation he is just honest.

2. Arnold has realized that the decision to tell other people the truth (= letting them into his life) is a good thing, because it gives them a chance to be helpful, sympathetic, to show their true feelings and become your friends.

3. – If he had worn a new suit to the dance he would just have looked normal and not "radioactive".
   – If Penelope's father hadn't allowed her to go along to the diner, nobody would know about Arnold's poverty still.

4. (Extra) a) Individual answers

b) "Yes": Arnold is a traitor to his tribe because he mostly thinks about his own future. Instead of that, he could organize some sort of protest on the rez to start better schooling conditions for the Indians there, for example. (against the background of rez life, not very realistic, however!)
   "No": He isn't a traitor, because the way things are, he can only help to change the living conditions of his tribe in the long run if he gets a good education/job and maybe has enough influence to help his people later on.

5. It means that he doesn't feel he really belongs to Wellpinit any more because he decided to leave his rez (because it couldn't provide him with the one thing he considered important for his future: a good education). However, he also doesn't feel that he belongs to Reardan neither, he feels like an outsider there in many ways (family background, social class, poverty, …). So he is 'in-between' and not completely at home in either place.

6. Gordy explains to Arnold that in former times communities were dependent on trust between individuals within the group in order to survive the threats and dangers from outside (p. 121, ll. 33/34). Arnold calls himself a "weird" person, and Gordy considers himself to be the same (p. 122, ll. 7/8). This means that the two are members of the "tribe of the weird".

7. (Extra) Rowdy and Gordy are two people J./A. likes, feels very close to and considers to be his friends. He would like the two to meet and get on with each other. He also dreams that the three of them would become a team that would be able to successfully and miraculously change the world (with regard to "truth, justice and the Native American Way", p. 121, ll. 17/18). The cartoon on p. 94 shows that Junior/Arnold already sees himself and Rowdy as "superheroes".

8. (Extra) Clichés mentioned on p. 111, ll. 1–16: people at Reardan assume that all Spokane Indians must be rich because they think they make a lot of money from the casino on the reservation; they also think the government gives a lot of money to Indians.
   Facts about Native American life on the reservation mentioned in the novel: the casino is mismanaged, and misplaced far away from the highway, so it cannot make money (p. 111, ll. 2–4); the Spokanes on the reservation are poor, with little hope of improving their living standards, and so there is an extremely high number of alcoholics leading to an extremely high number of accidents/deaths due to alcohol abuse; there is a low level of education, the reservation schools are badly equipped, leading to little chance of the young people finding well-paid jobs in the future.

NOTE   After reading the chapters, choose some of the tasks below to do individually, in pairs or in small groups. Any writing involved should go into your reading journal.

TASKS

1   How does Arnold Spirit cope with being poor?
   a) Look back (with the help of your content table) at instances in which Junior talks about his own or his tribe's poverty (cf. chapter 2).
   b) Arnold is confronted with the effects of his own poverty before and during the Winter Formal. With a partner, discuss his strategies to conceal his poverty (cartoon p. 110 + p. 113, ll. 17 ff. + pp. 114 ff.).
   c) List the events on the evening of the Winter Formal that eventually lead to Penelope's question "Are you poor?" (p. 117, l. 20).
   d) Compare the cartoon on page 118 with what actually happens at the end of the evening.

2   "If you let people into your life a little bit they can be pretty damn amazing" (p. 119, ll. 21/22). This is Junior's/Arnold's conclusion to the Winter Formal episode. Explain what he means, and discuss the lesson Junior has learned.

3   What if …? Write 5–8 conditional sentences about the events concerning the Winter Formal, e. g.:
   If Junior hadn't gone to the dance with Penelope, she would have gone with someone else. If he had worn a new suit to the dance, …

4   **(Extra)** Arnold explains to Gordy that Rowdy and the other Indians hate him because they think he is a traitor (p. 121, ll. 8, 20 ff.). Gordy comes up with an intellectual-sounding answer: "Well, life is a constant struggle between being an individual and being a member of the community." (p. 121, ll. 26–27)
   a) Discuss this statement with a partner.
   b) Give reasons why you think Junior/Arnold is or isn't a traitor to his tribe.

5   Explain Arnold's description of his situation when he says he is "half Indian in one place and half white in the other" (p. 109, l. 3).

6   Explain and discuss what Arnold means when he concludes "So we have a tribe of two" after his discussion with Gordy (p. 122, l. 9).

7   **(Extra)** "Or maybe Rowdy, Gordy, and I could become a superhero trio, fighting for truth, justice, and the Native American way." (p. 121, ll. 16–18). What gives Arnold such an idea? Discuss the wishes behind this idea, and make a short statement to put in your reading journal.

8   **(Extra)** The narrator mentions several clichés about Indians, e. g. p. 111, ll. 1–6. Point them out, and contrast them with some of the facts about Native American life on the reservation that you have learned from the novel so far. Keep this list handy (in your reading journal) so that you can add to it whenever new facts (or clichés) emerge.

End of Unit 4 ▶ Copymaster 13
Possible answers:
1. cf. summary on p. 27
2. "Thanksgiving":
   In this chapter, Junior describes how his family celebrates Thanksgiving; he wonders why Indians do so (see CM 11, 3b), and misses Rowdy's company more than ever on this day. When he sees that Rowdy doesn't refuse the cartoon he draws for him, he has his own personal reason for giving thanks.
   "Hunger Pains":
   Normally you have hunger pains when you haven't eaten for a long time, as a signal from your stomach that you need to eat. Here the title refers to Penelope being bulimic and making herself sick (or giving herself pain because she refuses to keep food inside her). It is also painful for A. to observe and learn about P.'s problems, her illness and the pain it causes her.
   "Rowdy Gives Me Advice About Love":
   This chapter describes yet another effort by J. to make contact with his best friend Rowdy. R. mails J. back saying that he is a racist for being in love with a white girl. The title is ironic, because R. definitely doesn't give J. any advice.

"Dance, Dance, Dance":
The chapter centres round the all-important Winter Formal dance at school, at which Arnold and Penelope manage to dance every single dance together, making this the best night of Arnold's life (p. 113, l. 4).
"Don't Trust Your Computer":
Junior's/Arnold's picture of his smiling face is answered by an e-mail of Rowdy's bare bottom, so the title could be continued as "… to smile back at you when you feel happy". The chapter continues with Gordy's serious comment about the importance of trust between individuals for communities (p. 121, ll. 33–34). At the end of the chapter, Arnold has established that he and Gordy, as weird outsiders, are a "tribe of two" – while his trust in Rowdy has been further challenged.
3. (Extra) Possible speculations:
   – Mary might write her novel.
   – Arnold will or will not be chosen for the basketball team.
   – Arnold's status at Reardan might be different now they all (?) know he is poor.
   – There must be some development/change in the relationship between J. and Rowdy, and J. and Penelope.

Unit 5 (pp. 123–163): Conflicting Loyalties

Summary
At the beginning of the sports season, Junior makes the varsity team at Reardan. He has to endure a serious defeat by Rowdy during their first match on the rez, when Reardan loses against Wellpinit for the first time. During the following winter months, both Junior's beloved grandmother and his father's best friend Eugene are killed in alcohol-related incidents. As a result, Junior becomes depressed and drops out of school. However, after 15–20 days he decides to go back, and is grateful when his new classmates stand by him against an insensitive teacher.

Chapters 19/20 (Sister/Junior the Sportsman) ▶ Copymaster 14
Possible answers:
1. a) Profile of Mary (continued):
   – is still looking for a job (dilemma: she can't get one because she is not experienced, but isn't given the chance to gain job experience)
   – has moved into a new "house" (a trailer that looks like a "TV dinner tray", p. 124, cartoon)
   – has started to write her life story
   b) "home" (OALD): (selection of relevant definitions)
   – the house or flat/apartment that you live in

   – the town, […] etc. that you come from or where you are living and that you feel you belong to
   – used to refer to a family living together, and the way it behaves
   – at home: comfortable and relaxed
   c) Mary had a house and a family, but she didn't feel at home on her reservation, that is why she lived in the basement; now she feels she belongs, as though she has 'come home'.
2. a) (selection) "court" (p. 126, l. 15), "bouncing and shooting" (l. 24), "varsity" (l. 27), "full-court one-on-one" (p. 128, l. 15), "quick guard" (l. 20), "power forward" (l. 21), "D" (= defense, p. 129, l. 6) "dribble" (l. 10), "shooter" (l. 23), "a 360" (p. 130, l. 11), "hoop" (l. 24), "jump shot" (l. 25), "layup" (l. 32), "rebounds" (p. 135, l. 15), "a pass" (l. 23), "free throws" (p. 136, l. 2).
   b) Individual answers
   c) Individual answers
   Websites:
   www.firstbasesports.com/basketball_glossary
   www.buzzle.com/articles/basketball-basic-rules-and-5positions-of-basketball.html
3. a) Junior/Arnold is frightened that he might be "cut from the team" (p. 125, l. 3) as he feels he is not good

TASKS **1** Write the unit summary.

2 Choose one of the chapters in unit 4 and explain its title.

3 **(Extra)** At this stage in the novel, there have been some positive developments. However, there is still something wrong in Junior's life. Discuss this with a partner. Make a few notes on what you expect the last third of the novel to deal with.

NOTE After reading the chapters, do some of the tasks below either individually, in pairs or in small groups, and put any writing in your reading journal.

TASKS

1 Mary

    a) Add to your profile of Mary, Junior's sister.

    b) Look up the term "home" in a monolingual dictionary.

    c) Comment on her title choice for her life story, "How to Run Away from Your House and Find Your Home" (p. 123, ll. 5/6).

2 **(Extra)** Basketball

    a) Go through Chapter 20 ("Reindeer Games") searching for terms from the field of basketball, and underline them / write them down.

    b) Look up the terms that you don't know so that you can picture the situation during the game better.

    c) Use these terms to explain some of the basic rules of basketball to the class. You might want to look on the Internet for some help.

3 Junior's decision to sign up

    a) What are Junior's/Arnold's feelings about trying out for the basketball team at Reardan? Discuss.

    b) Explain how his father influences his decision to sign up.

4 **(Extra)** "It was like something out of Shakespeare" (p. 132, l. 1). Explain Junior's comment by identifying the elements of drama in the match situation between Wellpinit and Reardan. Where do you see the climax? File your work in your reading journal.

5 Conflicting loyalties

    a) Look up the words "loyalty" and "conflict" in your dictionary or on the Internet.

    b) Explain the term "conflicting loyalties" in connection with Arnold Spirit's situation. Consider

    – his relation to his family,

    – his relation to the people on the rez (in particular Rowdy),

    – his relation to the Reardan team and its coach,

    – and any others you find interesting.

6 a) Make sure you understand all the words in the "emotions box":

"box of emotions"	
love	veneration
respect	amazement
admiration	hate
trust	fear
indifference	curiosity
loyalty	anger
despair	sympathy
affection	attraction
appreciation	disgust

b) Choose 2-3 emotions that Junior feels for each of the characters mentioned, and write them in the space provided below.

Mom   Dad   Grandma   Mary   Eugene   Rowdy

Junior's emotions

Penelope   Roger   Coach   Gordy   Penelope's father Earl

7 In a monolingual dictionary, look up the seven emotions you find most important, and for each of them write out the word families and collocations.
(For example: contempt > contemptuous, contemptible; with contempt, beneath contempt, hold in contempt, contempt for sth/sb ...)

8 Put this sheet in your reading journal and try to use the words and expressions in discussions and statements.

enough. He's scared of the "humiliation" (l. 4) in case he turns out to be not even "C squad" standard (l. 2).

b) His father encourages him by giving him the advice that "you have to dream big to get big" (p. 126, l. 7) meaning that you have to show courage and try something that you might not manage if you want to achieve something really important or 'big'.

4. (Extra)
   – two opposing teams centering around a protagonist and an antagonist
   – their supporters (fans) who stir up emotions
   – development (rising action) towards a highly emotional situation of confrontation which is more a battle than a sports match, ("He wanted to kill me, face-to-face", p. 133, l. 27), Arnold/Junior is injured when a quarter is thrown at him; gets stitches in forehead on site so he can continue playing.
   – climax: Rowdy gives Arnold/Junior a concussion, and he blacks out.
   – falling action: reconstructing events and telling stories with his coach

5. a) "loyalty" (OALD): "the quality of being faithful in your support of sb/sth";
   "conflict" (OALD): "a situation in which people, groups or countries are involved in a serious disagreement or argument"

   b) Conflicting loyalties in connection with Arnold Spirit's situation:
   – he loves his family and is proud of them, but they cannot provide him with the necessary support (money, reliability, help …) to fit in at Reardan
   – he feels at home on the rez and feels part of his Indian tribe, but he leaves them in order to get a better education, and ensure a better future for himself than they were able to achieve.
   – Rowdy is his best friend, he loves and trusts him, but he has to leave him behind, he even has to play basketball matches against him.

6. Individual answers
7. Individual answers
8. Individual answers

Chapters 21–23 (Red vs. White) ➤ Copymaster 15
Possible answers:

1. a) It is a beautiful present because his father didn't spend the (last of his) money on drinking – as he has often done before – in order to give his son a Christmas present. It is ugly because Junior's father's alcohol addiction is so strong that he had to keep it in his boot to stop himself from spending it – as a result it is wet, wrinkled, dirty and smelly and is a symbol of his father's problems ("Man, that thing smelled like booze and fear and failure", p. 139, ll. 5/6).

   b) Junior feels close to his father but upset and hurt at

the same time ("""… the man who had broken my heart again", p. 138, l. 14).

2. (Extra) a) "Partridge in a pear tree" is the (repeated) first verse of the famous English Christmas carol "The Twelve Days of Christmas": (extract)

   > On the first day of Christmas,
   > My true love sent to me
   > A partridge in a pear tree.
   >
   > On the second day of Christmas,
   > My true love sent to me
   > Two turtle doves,
   > And a partridge in a pear tree.
   >
   > On the third day of Christmas,
   > My true love sent to me
   > Three French hens,
   > Two turtle doves,
   > And a partridge in a pear tree.

   (From: www.englishbox.de)

   b) The song is about (quite extravagant) Christmas gifts from a lover to his "true love". Junior's father also gives his son an unexpected Christmas gift to express his love for him on this special occasion.

3. In Reardan, kids get ignored by their parents, parents don't seem to be interested in their children, they don't attend their activities such as sports events etc., parents (fathers in particular) don't know their children's friends, spend little or no time with their children ("I've learned that white people, especially fathers, are good at hiding in plain sight", p. 141, ll. 20/21).
   On the rez, "Everybody knows everybody" (p. 141, ll. 16/17), parents do "great parenting" (p. 140, l. 17) despite all their problems ("drinking" and being "eccentric", p. 141, l. 1), all families and family members are "really close to each other" (p. 141, l. 16).
   Possible reasons: parents at Reardan find it important to earn a lot of money, be successful at their jobs, maintain their social and living standards, have big houses where you can choose whether or not to see others or be close to them, maybe they think their children are looked after in school; on the rez parents have more time (unemployment), a different tradition, several generations living closely together so they are 'forced' to be close to one another, different ideas on education and family life.

4. a) Junior's grandmother has been described before as a wise, clever woman (e. g. her advice on how to treat Roger), is well-respected, known and loved in the community, knows all about Indian culture. New information here: tolerance is her greatest gift (including towards gay people), open-minded towards all new people and new experiences (p. 143, ll. 7 ff.).

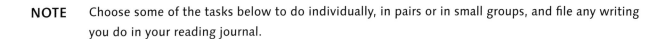

> **Copymaster 15** | Chapters 21-23 – Red vs. White

NOTE   Choose some of the tasks below to do individually, in pairs or in small groups, and file any writing you do in your reading journal.

TASKS

1 The Christmas present

    a) Junior calls the Christmas present that he belatedly receives from his father "a beautiful and ugly thing" (p. 139, l. 14). Explain what he means.

    b) Write a short statement about Junior's relationship to his father to put in your reading journal.

2 (Extra) Title of chapter 21

    a) Research the phrase "partridge in a pear tree". Where does it come from?

    b) Explain the choice of title for this chapter (see also note on p. 125).

3 Sum up the differences in family and community feelings in Reardan and on the rez that Junior mentions, and discuss possible reasons for these differences.

4 Junior's grandmother

    a) Write a profile of Junior's grandmother based on the information in chapter 22 as well as what you already knew about her before reading this.

    b) Discuss the tragic irony of her being killed by a drunk driver.

5 (Extra) Explain the cartoon on page 143 in connection with the text (p. 143, l. 18 – p. 144, l. 3).

6 Look up the word "wake" in a dictionary, and explain to a partner how you imagine a wake.

7 Compile a list of words and expressions to do with funerals and wakes.

8 Report the events at the grandmother's funeral for a local newspaper.

9 (Extra) "Heaven"

    a) Explain the drawing on page 154.

    b) With a partner, write down your ideas and impressions as a short story for your reading journal.

b) The tragedy lies in the irony that a woman who never drank any alcohol herself (p. 145, l. 24), is killed by a drunk driver. So in the end even her death is alcohol-related.

5. (Extra) Junior tries to picture the fact that his grandma is so open-minded that she even talks to invisible people on the chance that they really do exist and deserve to be treated in a friendly way. She thinks we are too narrow-minded and might be mistaken just as scientists did not originally believe that mountain gorillas existed but eventually had to admit to their mistake once it was proven true.

6. "wake" (OALD): An occasion before a funeral when people gather to remember the dead person, traditionally held at night.

7. widow/widower, to mourn, mourner, loved ones, to be bereaved, to cry, to wail, grief, to grieve (relatives);
to bury s.o., priest, religious ceremony, hymn, sermon, "ashes to ashes, clay to clay", chapel, grave, graveyard (services)

8. ***Tears And Laughter at Grandmother Spirit's Funeral***
Yesterday there was a gathering of over 2000 Indians as well as some white people on the Wellpinit football field in honour of the woman known as Grandmother Spirit, who died in a recent car accident. The funeral ceremony had to be transferred from the Spokane Tribal Longhouse to the field in order to accommodate the great number of mourners. There were many who said Grandmother Spirit was one of the greatest Spokane Indians in history. As it is the tradition in Indian communities, many stories were told about her during the ceremony. After many hours of story-telling, a white stranger stood up and introduced himself as Ted, known to some as Billionaire Ted because of his considerable wealth. He was carrying a large suitcase ...

(further points to include: Ted's love of Indian lore, display of powwow dancing outfit, wanting to return it to its rightful owner, daughter's reaction ... laughter at Ted's humiliation)

9. (Extra) a) The drawing shows Junior's picture of the gateway to heaven as a sort of shop entrance door, where Grandma Spirit is already expected. It looks like a happy place where you can buy all the necessary equipment (halos, wings) to become an angel and where you might even meet your favourite star (Elvis).
b) "When Grandma Spirit approached the doorway to heaven, she was delighted to see that there were balloons out to welcome her. Before pushing the door open, she stopped to read the notices of all the heavenly things awaiting her inside ..."

Chapter 24 (The Little Pieces of Joy)
➤ **Copymaster 16**
Possible answers:

1. Eugene (cf. Unit 3) was like an "uncle" for Junior (p. 67, l. 10); he helped him in difficult situations (e. g. gave him lifts), was always friendly to him and seemed to be a very strong, always positive person who was liked by everybody (cf. p. 68, l. 1). Junior cannot accept the senselessness of his terrible and violent death (particularly as it happens so soon after his grandmother's death.). He feels "helpless and stupid" (p. 156, l. 3). This condition makes him want to read books and draw cartoons to cope.

2. "grief" (OALD): feeling of great sadness, especially when somebody dies, overcome with grief, grief- stricken, (to) grieve for/over sb/sth.
Synonyms for "grief": mourning, sadness, sorrow, agony, bereavement, distress, suffering. Synonyms for "to grieve": to mourn, to lament, to suffer, to wail, to weep.

3. (Extra) Medea is a play written by the Greek playwright Euripides (480 B.C.–406 B.C.). It is about the mytho-logical Greek hero Jason, and Medea, the mother of his two sons. They live in the Greek city of Corinth. Medea is not of Greek origin. In the past, she had to disown her family and even kill her brother in order to help Jason and come to Corinth with him. But because she is not Greek, Jason cannot marry her. Instead, he agrees to marry Creusa, the king's daughter, and bans Medea from his life, ordering her to leave their sons behind with him. Medea is so furious at his betrayal after all she went through to be with Jason in the first place, that she first kills Creusa and then her own two sons, saying that if she can't keep them, then Jason won't have them either. Finally, she leaves Corinth in a chariot drawn by dragons.
(From: www.historyforkids.org)

4. (Extra) Medea says: "What greater grief than the loss of one's native land?" (p. 158, ll. 8/9). Similarly, Arnold feels he had to give up his native land (the rez) in order to realize his dream of a better education and a more successful future. This often makes him feel sad because he has become a stranger in his hometown Wellpinit and he does not really feel accepted in Reardan either.

5. After his classmates demonstrated their solidarity with Arnold because they want to show their disapproval of the way the social studies teacher behaved towards him, Arnold realizes that it doesn't really matter if people have a certain skin colour or belong to an Indian tribe or not. The only thing that really matters for him is if they can show their sympathy and understanding for fellow humans or not (in his words: if they are "assholes" or not, p. 161, ll. 15/16).

NOTE Choose a few of the tasks below to do individually, in pairs or in small groups, and include any writing in your reading journal.

TASKS

1 Explain what Eugene means to Junior and how his violent death affects Junior's life.

2 Look up the word "grief" and find more words or phrases that express similar feelings. Use a dictionary.

3 **(Extra)** Look up Euripides and Medea on the Internet and give a short presentation of Medea's story.

4 **(Extra)** Explain why Arnold is so fascinated by what Euripides's Medea says about grief.

5 Explain Arnold's realization that "the world is only broken into two tribes" (p. 161, l. 15) in the context of what happened in the social studies classroom.

6 Arnold Spirit makes several lists of "the little pieces of joy" in his life (pp. 161 ff.). Make up some lists of your own and include them in your reading journal.

End of Unit 5

TASKS

1 Write the unit summary.

2 **(Extra)** Arnold has gone through hard times, but he has started to cope better with his new situation. What is still missing in his life to give him further peace of mind? Talk to a partner about this and file the notes you make.

6. Possible lists are "People I feel close to"; "Things I like doing best"; "Films that impressed me most"; (see Arnold's lists on people, foods, books, musicians, basketball players and other sports people).

End of Unit 5 ➤ Copymaster 16
Possible answers:
1. cf. summary on p. 34
2. (Extra) Possible things missing: making up (or not) with Rowdy, revenge against the Wellpinit basketball team, Mary's successful future e.g. writing her book, getting a job (or not)

Unit 6 (pp. 164–210): Coming to Terms

Summary

Junior is determined to make good the humiliation of Reardan's defeat against Wellpinit in the rematch. With seemingly superhuman powers he actually manages to beat Rowdy in the first seconds of the game and subsequently leads Reardan to victory against their opponents. However, ultimately Junior is ashamed of having led a white team to victory against his own people, who are born losers anyway. Shortly afterwards, Junior's sister Mary, who had also left the reservation and married into a different tribe, burns to death with her husband in their mobile home after a party. Once more Junior has to confront the question of whether he is to blame for all these deaths because of his divided loyalties. At the end of the school year, he and Rowdy finally become friends again because both realize that people are different and have to follow different paths in their lives.

Chapters 25/26 (The Match) ➤ Copymaster 17
Possible answers:
1. On the reservation, nobody ever believed in Junior's abilities, and so he was never forced to prove them – except his intellectual skills, which nobody on the rez was interested in anyway. At Reardan, Coach as well as his team-mates see Arnold's potential and expect him to be good (p. 165, ll. 1–3). This builds up his confidence, and his skills improve as a result. He knows that he is an essential part of a good team ("none of them could shoot like me", p. 164, l. 8). Before the rematch with Wellpinit, Coach encourages him to guard Rowdy, the best Wellpinit player. He tells him repeatedly that he can do it (cf. p. 172), so that Arnold starts to believe he can, too. Eventually Arnold feels strong enough to do the job he is expected to do for his team.
2. (Extra) Individual answers
3. – His former best friend Rowdy gave him a concussion and saw to it that Reardan was utterly defeated in the first match.
   – Arnold has become a confident player and integral member of the Reardan team, which is known to be a winning team.
   – Arnold/Junior feels he must take revenge on Rowdy

for the humiliation suffered after the last match.
   – The night of the rematch is "the most important" one for Arnold because he wants to prove both his strength and his desire to win to the people at Reardan (and at Wellpinit, cf. p. 170, ll. 12 ff).
4. Individual answers
5. (Extra) Junior wants "revenge" (p. 179, l. 18) on the Wellpinit Redskins, and especially on Rowdy for humiliating him in the first match – but Junior also wants Rowdy to be his friend again. However, his classmates at Reardan have become his friends and without their support he wouldn't be able to play as well as he does. When the game is over, he first cheers along with the Reardan team and their followers, thinking that they have defeated the stronger ones as David defeated the giant Goliath (p. 178). And then he suddenly realizes that in fact Reardan is Goliath and Wellpinit is David, the underdog. While Rowdy as an individual may indeed be stronger than Arnold, as a team the Reardan players are the giants while Wellpinit is a team that usually loses in life because it comes from the reservation. This realization makes Junior cry "tears of shame" (p. 179, l. 28), and he knows that he has broken his "best friend's heart" (l. 29).
6. Men and boys are often considered "sissies" if they cry, especially in public, but sports is officially their emotional domain, so in connection with sports everyone seems to understand their emotions.
   Note: A comment could consider whether this is true in all cultures, and whether it is fair on boys if they are not supposed to show emotions.

Chapter 27 (Mary's Death) ➤ Copymaster 18
Possible answers:
1. Life on the reservation is very restricted, and most adults resort to alcohol to forget their unemployment, poverty and hopelessness. Alcohol in combination with frustration leads to violence, or to fatal accidents, and all this occurs regularly on the reservation, while the white communities do not suffer so massively from the problems that cause alcoholism and therefore do not suffer the consequences of alcoholism.

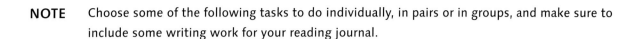

NOTE Choose some of the following tasks to do individually, in pairs or in groups, and make sure to include some writing work for your reading journal.

TASKS

1 "The power of expectations" (p. 165, l. 6): Explain how the expectations that different people have of Junior influence his basketball performance. Include the beginning of the match (pp. 172/173) in your explanation.

2 **(Extra)** Can you think of a situation in which people's expectations influenced your performance? Talk about this to a partner, or a small group, or write it down and include it in your reading journal.

3 Discuss the importance of winning the rematch against Wellpinit for Arnold Spirit as a member of the Reardan team.

4 In a small group, turn the narrative episode of the television crew interviewing Arnold into a short dramatic sketch. Practise acting it before you perform it for the whole class. Decide whether you want this to be a serious or a funny incident, and act accordingly.

5 **(Extra)** Friendship, fame – and "tears of shame" (p. 179, l. 28). Explain the connection for Arnold Spirit in the context of the rematch and its consequences.

6 Comment on the statement that it is only after defeat in sports that "men and boys get to cry and not get punched in the face" (p. 180, ll. 9–10).

NOTE   Choose one or two of the following tasks to discuss in pairs or groups, and include any written work in your reading journal.

TASKS   1   "I'm fourteen years old and I've been to forty-two funerals." (p. 182, l. 7). Explain why Junior says that this sobering fact is one of the biggest differences between Indians and white people.

2   **(Extra)** "Every unhappy family is unhappy in its own way" (p. 183, ll. 2/3)
   a) Discuss the quotation from Tolstoy's 19th century novel *Anna Karenina* illustrating it with examples you can think of outside the story of Arnold Spirit.
   b) State why Arnold says that for Indians this is simply not true.

3   Imagine the guidance counselor, Miss Warren, writes a diary entry about how she had to tell Arnold about the death of his sister. Write this (with a partner, if you like), and put it in your reading journal.

4   Rowdy accuses Junior of having killed Mary, and he agrees. Explain and comment. What does this particular grief mean for Rowdy? What does it mean for Junior? What can it mean for the relationship of the two teenagers?

2. (Extra) a) Tolstoy's narrator claims that unhappiness is an individual thing, and that one family's unhappiness comes from different sources to any other family's. Such sources of unhappiness can be an unhappy marriage, childlessness, a disabled child, a death in the family, the failure to get the job one wanted, illness etc.

b) Junior has experienced that in his community all unhappiness comes from the same source, i.e. alcohol. All the deaths he has been confronted with can be traced to that one source, the worst for him being his sister Mary's burning in her mobile home too drunk to even notice the fire.

3. (model beginning)
"Had to go through something terrible in the office today. Got a call that Arnold Spirit's older sister had died in a fire, and I had to be the one to inform him. Horrible. I simply hugged him at first because I couldn't talk, but then I had to say it, and he played dumb and acted like he didn't understand me. Eventually he wanted me to say exactly how she died …"

4. Junior feels that Rowdy must be right, because if he hadn't taken the initiative and (partly) left the reservation, Mary might still be there and alive (cf. p. 192, ll. 33 ff.). Of course this is not a sensible conclusion, because it would mean that people are not supposed to leave the life they have to look for a better, or at least different life. Besides, Mary could have got into any number of alcohol-related (or not) accidents even if she had stayed at Wellpinit, so this accusation cannot be valid. Rowdy is so emotional because it is a way for him to voice his fury and grief over his best friend leaving him. He knows how much Junior loved his sister, so he knows exactly what to say to hit Junior's nerve, without having to confront his own feelings of being the weak victim of betrayal (cf. p. 191, ll. 28 ff.). But it seems that the time is not ripe for their reunion yet, as Rowdy cries out that he hates Junior (p. 193, l. 2).

Chapters 28–30 (Remembering) ▶ Copymaster 19
Possible answers:
1. The top line features Arnold's name not as that of a student, but as if he were an old-fashioned adult academic (Mr., Esq., PhD). At the same time, using an asterisk he makes fun of the academic title PhD ("pretty hot dude") in the margin. Below this is a play on the school's name: Rear + dumb (for the 2nd syllable "dan"), to which Arnold has added the adjective "high" in brackets. Next to it is the Indian mascot of the school, making panting noises as though he has just run a race. Another play on words makes up the next line, where "Freshman" has become "fresh mint" with the drawing of a mint candy next to it. A list of the subjects and grades follows, which may well be a correct rendering

of Arnold's achievements. The B + in "Geology" might allude to the incident with the Science teacher (and the subject probably is Science, not Geology). The B– in what is probably meant to be woodwork class reflects the physical handicaps Arnold has told us of, such as bad eyesight and oversized hands (p. 7, ll. 6–14). The whole cartoon reflects Arnold's/Junior's joy at having completed his first year at Reardan and at being accepted by the others. If he didn't feel like this, he would not be able to make fun of his report card in that way.

2. Reservations were originally meant as a kind of prison camp for Native American tribal members (cf. p. 198, ll. 19–23), but today Indians just see them as their homelands and hardly ever want to leave them, they even feel betrayed by individuals who do leave. Junior knows that leaving the rez might be dangerous, maybe even kill him as it killed his sister, but he also knows that staying on the rez would certainly kill him because it would have frustrated him to live there and he would probably have turned to alcohol and eventually be killed by it.

3. (Extra) Individual answers

4. Arnold realizes that there are many different ways of defining your own identity, and because of that, he will always have somebody to fall back on from one of the tribes to which he belongs.

5. (Extra) When Junior points out the beauty of his homeland, the rez, he is making it clear that he is still a member of the tribe that lives there, and that this is his real home, even though he has become only a "part-time Indian" through his transfer to the white school. His childhood memories of fun times with Rowdy on the rez make their friendship come alive again for Junior and remind the reader that the most important thing in Junior's life is still missing at the end of his school year, i.e. being best friends with Rowdy.
The memory of successfully climbing the pine tree with Rowdy is paralleled with Junior's present and his successful "survival" of his freshman year at Reardan. It also brings home to us, the readers, that he was probably destined to confront challenges from the start (cf. also what Mr. P says, p. 44, ll. 2–6).

6. (Extra) Individual work

End of Unit 6 ▶ Copymaster 19
Possible answers:
1. cf. summary on p. 42
2. (Extra) It could be called a happy ending because the two best friends are reunited once more. However it is also an open, ambiguous ending because, although they have reached an understanding for the moment, their futures will undoubtedly go in very different directions, and it is not yet clear how stable or long-lasting this new-found peace will be.

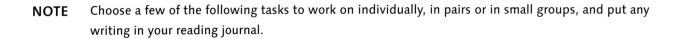

NOTE   Choose a few of the following tasks to work on individually, in pairs or in small groups, and put any writing in your reading journal.

TASKS   1   Describe the "report card" on page 196 and explain what it means in the context of Arnold Spirit's story.

2   Sum up Junior's thoughts about Indian Reservations, and discuss his realization that his attempt to leave the rez might kill him, but staying would have killed him, too (p. 198, ll. 9–10).

3   **(Extra)** In your reading journal, write an essay entitled "Why Arnold Spirit had to leave the rez".

4   Study Arnold's list of tribes he belongs to, and explain why this list makes him think he will "be okay" (cf. p. 199, l. 11).

5   **(Extra)** The last chapter begins with a description of the beauty of the reservation, and goes on to tell a story about Rowdy and Junior that happened when they were both a lot younger. Discuss with a partner (or in class) what the effect of such a digression near the end of the novel is, and why the author might have wanted to achieve this effect.

6   **(Extra)** Tell your classmates the story about "Stupid Horse" without reading out anything, i. e. as 'oral history'.

End of Unit 6

TASKS   1   Write the unit summary.

2   **(Extra)** How do you feel about the ending? Do you think the story has a happy ending or a more open, ambiguous one? Write a statement and put it in your reading journal.

Post-reading Activities

Looking Back at the Novel ➤ Copymaster 20

Possible answers:

1. a) Individual work

   b) The point of view of a 14-year-old who reduces the plot to "action and emotion" makes it seem like a friend talking to you.

   c) e. g. listening to Penelope in the girls' bathroom; the dog's death; Roger offering to pay for the meal after the dance; Junior's language (very colloquial register, even slang), the details mentioned, the mental images produced while reading, the cartoons

   d) (Extra) Individual answers

2. Individual answers

3. e.g. not really just about school life; really about conflicting loyalties and direct and honest accounts of emotions, including his failures; unexpected turns (when Roger doesn't fight back, death of Mary etc.); scope of topics including life and deaths on the rez; insights into unfamiliar ways of life; back and forth between two "cultures"…

4. a) Individual answers

   b) and c) Possible role card notes for Penelope coming back (from the Great Wall of China) to give a talk to students at Reardan High:

   – self-confident architect (works for a firm) coming back from a holiday trip to China

   – remembers talking about dreams with Arnold Spirit as a teenager

   – wanted to dream big, even if not realistic

   – went to Stanford to study architecture, worked hard, left Reardan behind (but likes coming back to visit)

   – Great Wall of China was a childhood dream, because so far away and so famous. Great experience!

   – advises school kids to dream big for themselves, make sth. of their lives

   (cf. pp. 102 f. for more material)

5. Individual answers

Written Tests

Suggestions for testing students' reading and writing skills in connection with the novel

Written Test 1 (Dealing With an Excerpt from the Novel) ➤ Copymaster 21

Note: This type of test is suitable for testing students' abilities to deal with a fictional text whose context they are familiar with. It can be used in case the date for a "Klausur" precedes the time by which students can be expected to show familiarity with the complete novel and its topics.

Possible answers:

1. The narrator, Junior, has transferred from the reservation school to a white school in Reardan. During his first days there, he is taunted and insulted for being an Indian, so he punches Roger, the leader of his tormentors, in the nose. When Roger not only does not fight back, but actually shows him some respect afterwards, Junior realizes that he has won a kind of victory, but this does not mean that he has made friends, as the excerpt shows. They all simply leave him alone now. He becomes depressed, as he has lost his friends on the reservation by transferring to a white school, and so he feels as lonely in the "Indian" part of his life as he does at his new school in Reardan.

2. The passage is told by the same first-person narrator who tells all the events in the novel, i. e. by the protagonist, Junior, himself. He uses very informal language, underlining his feelings with lists of synonyms of "nothing", repetitions and exaggerations ("zitty and lonely", "less than less than less"; "up and down, up and down") and involving the reader as if in a conversation ("Well, no, …"; "In fact, if you think …"; "And I know you're thinking …", "And okay, maybe …"). One image sticks out (and also gets a cartoon), which is that of the "zit", which he identifies with. The effect is that teenage readers will especially be able to empathize with the narrator/protagonist when he conjures up mental images of being lonely in a school environment.

3. Junior still lives with his family on the reservation, where he considers himself to be an Indian. When he leaves the reservation every morning to go to Reardan, he knows that he is turning his back on his friends on the rez in order to establish a better life for himself, and he knows that they all think he is betraying them. One thing that clearly does change every morning is his name. On the rez, he is "Junior", while at Reardan he is known as "Arnold". It is not a total change – or even loss – of identity, because "Arnold" is indeed his given name, but it does affect him. It is interesting to note that he calls the change that happens on his way to school

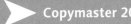

NOTE   Choose one or two of the following activities/tasks and make sure you include the results in your reading journal.

TASKS   **1**   Dealing with part of a review

a) Read the following final paragraph of a review.

"For fifteen years now, Sherman Alexie has explored the struggle to survive between the grinding plates[1] of the Indian and white worlds. He's done it through various characters and genres, but *The Absolutely True Diary* may be his best work yet. Working in the voice of a fourteen-year-old forces Alexie to strip everything down to action and emotion, so that reading becomes more like listening to your smart, funny best friend recount[2] his day while waiting after school for a ride home."

(From: Bruce Barcott, "Off the Rez", in NYTimes online, *11-11-2007)*

[1] *grinding plates:* Schleifscheibe   [2] *recount sth.* = tell about sth.

b) Explain what the reviewer finds so convincing about the novel.

c) Talk with a partner (or in a small group) about your favourite moments in the novel which you think illustrate the reviewer's argument.

d) **(Extra)** Write your own short review of the novel for your reading journal, using the examples you talked about as material.

2   Why read "The Absolutely True Diary of a Part-Time Indian"?

Think: On three separate cards (or slips of paper) write down three arguments about why you personally think the novel is worth reading. (Alternatively, if you did not enjoy reading it, write down three arguments against reading the novel.)

Pair: Place your six argument cards in front of you, and compare them. If you have similar, or even identical arguments put the cards together, or discard one of them.

Share: In groups of six, tell each other the outcome of your pair work, and again compare the remaining arguments, discarding any doubles. Discuss the order of importance and prepare a short statement to give the whole class.

3   The structure of the novel

The novel consists of a diary which mainly covers the span of the protagonist's first year of high school.

Analyse how the author manages to grab your attention and keep you turning the pages of a book about school life.

4   Twenty years later: Projecting the characters into the future

a) Brainstorm how you imagine Penelope, Rowdy or Arnold/Junior twenty years in the future (e. g. Penelope as a tourist on the Great Wall of China? Rowdy as a basketball pro? Arnold as a social scientist?). Feel free to choose your own scenarios!

b) With a partner, prepare a role card (or profile) for your chosen character.

c) In groups, choose one of the following settings and prepare a presentation:
   – the character is being interviewed on TV (invent a situation and practise the interview)
   – the character is invited back to Reardan High to give a talk to students (prepare a speech)
   – **(Extra)** Two of the characters are invited to a talk show. Invent an appropriate setting (and topic!) and act out part of the talk show.

5 Spokane Indians beyond the novel: a webquest
   Go to the following website and answer the questions below about the history of the Spokane Indians: www.wellpinit.wednet.edu/sal-qa/qa.php
   (Of course, if you like, you may also find answers to any other questions.)

Questions:
   1. Who are the Spokane Indians?
   2. Where did the Spokane tribe come from?
   3. What did the Spokanes wear, and what did they look like?
   4. Did the Spokane tribe live in towns? What were their houses like?
   5. What was the guardian-spirit quest?
   6. What was their art like?
   7. What are current Native American issues?

NAME: **CLASS:**   **WRITTEN TEST NO:**   **DATE:**

Excerpt from "The Absolutely True Diary of a Part-Time Indian" by Sherman Alexie

I walked like a zombie the next few weeks in Reardan.

Well, no, that's not exactly the right description.

I mean, if I'd been walking around like a zombie, I might have been scary. So, no, I wasn't a zombie, not at all.

Because you can't ignore a zombie. So that made me, well, it made me nothing.

5   Zero.

Zilch.

Nada.

In fact, if you think of everybody with a body, soul, and brain as a human, then I was the opposite of human.

It was the loneliest time of my life.

10 And whenever I get lonely, I grow a big zit on the end of my nose.

If things didn't get better soon, I was going to turn into one giant walking talking zit.

A strange thing was happening to me.

Zitty and lonely, I woke up on the reservation as an Indian, and somewhere on the road to Reardan,

I became something less than Indian.

15 And once I arrived at Reardan, I became something less than less than less than Indian.

Those white kids didn't talk to me.

They barely looked at me.

Well, Roger would nod his head at me, but he didn't socialize with me or anything. I wondered if maybe I should punch everybody in the face. Maybe they'd all pay attention to me then.

20 I just walked from class to class alone; I sat at lunch alone; during PE I stood in the corner of the gym and played catch with myself. I just tossed a basketball up and down, up and down, up and down.

And I know you're thinking, "Okay, Mr. Sad Sack, how many ways are you going to tell us how depressed you were?"

And, okay, maybe I'm overstating my case. Maybe I'm exaggerating.

(From: Sherman Alexie: "The Absolutely True Diary of a Part-Time Indian", beginning of chapter 12, pp. 76/77)

TASKS   1 (Comprehension) Briefly sum up the events that lead to this moment in the novel and say what is described in this excerpt.

2 (Analysis) Analyse the way Junior tells us about his feelings in this episode. What is the effect on you?

3 (Comment) From what you have learned about Junior so far, comment on the following quote:

"Zitty and lonely, I woke up on the reservation as an Indian and somewhere on the road to Reardan, I became something less than Indian" (ll. 13/14).

becoming "something less than Indian", i. e. at this stage he views the change as a loss with no gain as yet. It is definitely a very difficult time for him.

Written Test 2 (Dealing With a Review of the Novel)
➤ **Copymaster 22**
Possible answers:
1. a) The reviewer shows conflicting attitudes towards the novel. While she is sure that readers will not be able to put it down, she also warns that it is not always nice to read because the sex and violence might disgust readers and the tragic events will make them sad, but all in all the adventures of the protagonist will thrill them, especially because they are semi-autobiographical.
   b) In the middle of the review presented here there is a gap, in which almost certainly the writer summed up the main elements of the plot. It could probably go like this: "Arnold Spirit, called Junior by his Native American family and friends on the reservation, was born with water on the brain and throughout his childhood had to overcome many physical difficulties. But he is smart and sensitive, and one day he decides to give himself hope of a brighter future by transferring from the reservation school to a white school in Reardan, where he is the only Indian student. After a difficult time fighting to be accepted by his peers, he eventually makes friends and even dates the most popular girl in his class, Penelope. At the same time, his reservation friends, in particular his long-time best friend Rowdy, consider him a traitor and turn their backs on him. There are several showdowns between Junior and Rowdy, since each boy is on his school's basketball team and fights hard to win the matches between the schools."
2. "a magnanimous stew of reality and hope":
   The "ingredients" of a stew are cooked together and cannot be separated, just like the different elements of the novel. The whole is a very generous mixture, with "reality" referring to the hard life on the reservation and the many deaths and harsh truths about life which the protagonist has to cope with. "Hope" refers to the encouragement given to Junior by many of the adults in his life which give him the strength to survive his freshman year at Reardan.
   "sex and violence rear their ugly heads":
   This is an idiom meaning that sex and violence are unpleasant aspects within the novel. Sex is a topic because the protagonist is a 14-year-old boy, and he talks about masturbating, making out, erections in different situations, including his girlfriend's father's dirty imagination. Violence is shown in the beatings and abuse Junior suffers on the reservation, as well as Rowdy's aggressive tendencies, which stem from his father's frequent drunken mistreatment of him and his mother. One of the most violent scenes is Rowdy's attack

on Junior during their first basketball match on opposing teams.
"adolescent wanderings":
("wanderings" OALD: journeys from place to place, usu. with no special purpose.) Here the part-time Indian life of Junior/Arnold is referred to; a life in which he "wanders" between Reardan and "the rez", gaining different (adolescent) experience, such as falling in love with Penelope, being seen as stylish in his father's old suit at the Winter Formal, admitting his poverty after a night of partying, having to bury several close family members and friends on the rez, making, losing and remaking friends.
"great flowering words of encouragement":
These words come from J.'s Dad, from Mr. P, from Eugene, and especially from Coach. Since they are given so much room, the reviewer calls them "great" and "flowering", as if they were blossoms on a tree.
"Hope is indeed the thing with feathers":
A quotation from a 19th century poem by Emily Dickinson, used here to emphasize the fact that hope is a big aspect of the novel and something which redeems the more depressing parts. The feathers could also refer to the feathers on an Indian warrior's arrow (to make it fly faster), or on a bird's wings, which would suggest the idea of hope flying in a particular direction – or it might be a general allusion to the feathers on an Indian chief's headdress.
3. Individual answers
   Note: Arguments must be supported from the text, from personal reading experience, and must be specific.

NAME: **CLASS:**   **WRITTEN TEST NO:**   **DATE:**

Extract from a review of "The Absolutely True Diary of a Part-Time Indian"

When was the last time a book not only made you a little bit nauseous but excited as well?
The National Book Award-winning novel "The Absolutely True Diary of a Part-Time Indian" by Sherman Alexie is such a magnanimous stew of reality and hope – and the particular traumatic existence of a reservation teen in contemporary America – that you can't possibly put it down, no matter how sad, disgusted or freaked

5   out it makes you. […]
By the end of the book, you are entirely inside Junior's oversized head. I found it hard to shake him, his world and his travails when I turned the last page. There is something in the force of Alexie's description that captures your heart, even while some of his raunchiest statements can turn your stomach. Boys of this age will be boys of this age, regardless of race or economic class. There is much to recommend here, but one word of warning:

10 sex and violence rear their ugly heads as much as deep and unabiding sorrow and great flowering words of encouragement.
This is a book that delves into every possible aspect of one boy's adolescent wanderings. The fact that Alexie actually encountered such incidents in real life only serves to make the narrative that much more imposing. Knowing that he fought a successful fight against all the things that oppressed him as a kid gives "The

15 Absolutely True Diary of a Part-Time Indian" even greater resonance. Hope is indeed the thing with feathers.

(248 words)

(From: "The Absolutely True Diary of a Part-Time Indian" by Sherman Alexie, reviewed by Jana Siciliano – extracts, www.teenreads.com/reviews/9780316013697.asp)

1 *nauseous:* feeling as if you want to vomit   3 *magnanimous (fml):* generous   *stew: a dish of meat and vegetables cooked together in a pot*
7 *travails (literary):* unpleasant experiences   8 *raunchy (infml):* sexy   10 *sth. rears its ugly head (idm.):* sth unpleasant is shown
12 *delve into sth:* try hard to find out more about sth.   15 *"Hope is the thing with feathers":* first line of a poem by Emily Dickinson
(1830-1886)

TASKS   1 (Comprehension) Looking at content
        a) Sum up the reviewer's opinion of the novel.
        b) In the middle there is a gap "[…]". Consider what essential part of a review is missing and fill in what you think belongs there.

     2 The reviewer uses some images and metaphors to show us her impression of the novel, i. e. "a magnanimous stew of reality and hope", "sex and violence rear their ugly heads", "adolescent wanderings", "great flowering words of encouragement", "Hope is indeed the thing with feathers".
        Choose two of them and explain them with reference to details from the novel as you remember them.

     3 Finally, write a short statement why or why not you would recommend this novel to other teenagers.